Futures of Socialism

Futures of Socialism

The Pandemic and the Post-Corbyn Era

Edited by
Grace Blakeley

VERSO
London • New York

First published by Verso 2020

Certain chapters have been previously published as follows: Chapter 9, 'If Hopes
Were Dupes, Fears May Be Liars', *New Socialist*, 4 March 2020; Chapter 11, 'The
Coronavirus and the Crisis this Time', *Bullet*, 10 April 2020; Chapter 12, 'Anti-
Racism Requires More Than Passive Sympathy', *Guardian*, 8 June 2020; Chapter
14, 'Hunger Gnaws at the Edges of the World', *Newsletter of the Tricontinental:
Institute for Social Research*, no. 20, 14 May 2020; Chapter 17, 'Making It Count:
Resisting the Authority of Ignorance', *Ceasefire*, 10 June 2020; Chapter 25, 'As
One of Oxford's Few Black Professors, Let Me Tell You Why I Care about
Rhodes', *Guardian*, 12 June 2020.

1 3 5 7 9 10 8 6 4 2

Verso
UK: 6 Meard Street, London W1F 0EG
US: 20 Jay Street, Suite 1010, Brooklyn, NY 11201
versobooks.com

Verso is the imprint of New Left Books

ISBN-13: 978-1-83976-133-1
ISBN-13: 978-1-83976-134-8 (US EBK)
ISBN-13: 978-1-83976-135-5 (UK EBK)

British Library Cataloguing in Publication Data
A catalogue record for this book is available from the British Library

Library of Congress Cataloging-in-Publication Data
A catalog record for this book is available from the Library of Congress
Library of Congress Control Number: 2020943885

Typeset in Fournier by MJ & N Gavan, Truro, Cornwall
Printed and bound by CPI Group (UK) Ltd, Croydon, CR0 4YY

Contents

Introduction
Grace Blakeley

The last month of the 2010s dealt the British left a harrowing blow. For the second time in that decade, the Labour Party had been led into an early election by a democratic socialist leader with a radical policy platform. For the fourth time in that decade, the Party was defeated at the polls. While Corbyn's Labour won a higher share of the vote in 2019 than the Party had in 2010 or 2015, the consolidation of the right around Boris Johnson saw Labour gain the fewest seats since 1935. This collection of essays by leading thinkers, campaigners and activists from throughout the vibrant socialist movement that underpinned Corbyn's leadership is an attempt to learn some of the lessons of that defeat and chart a way forward for the left.

As the reader will soon discover, there remain disagreements between our contributors, which reflect divergent opinions within the wider movement. On the Party's Brexit position, the strengths or weaknesses of its manifesto and the strategic alliances that socialists should or should not have made, to name but a few issues, there is no consensus between the authors. This was a conscious decision: to have chosen contributions based on their adherence to a predetermined political line would have been to occlude real and important differences of opinion. And yet there also exists a striking degree of convergence, reflecting the powerful collective process of sense-making that has been undertaken in the short period since the election defeat. Our contributors agree on the need to strengthen and consolidate the progressive social forces that make up the wider left – forces such as the labour movement, the environmental movement and the feminist and anti-racist movements, to name but a few. Most cite the importance of ongoing democratisation within the Labour Party, and the stepping up of political education outside it. All are clear that, in the UK, the US and across Europe, the socialist movement is far stronger today than it was before the financial crisis – and also that we have a long way to go.

We do not have much time. As this book went to press, the world was entering perhaps the most significant social and economic crisis of our lifetimes, triggered by the spread of a novel coronavirus, declared a pandemic by the World Health Organisation in March 2020. Many of the contributors are clear that, in COVID-19, we face a unique existential threat for which our social, economic and political systems are woefully unprepared. Decades of neoliberal consensus have eroded the capacities of the state, now so desperately needed both to contain the spread of the virus and to treat those affected by it. In the UK, the weakening of our public services, our social safety net and our public infrastructure are all being exposed, as millions of workers are enduring hazardous conditions to meet the needs of those who are forced to remain at home.

The massive expansion in the size of the state necessary to

deal with this crisis was immediately recognised by many of the contributors not as a progressive development – an acceptance of the ideas put forward by socialists over the last several years – but as a reaction by the ruling classes to the threat posed to global capitalism by the pandemic. The speed with which our political leaders acted to support finance, big businesses and the wealthy stood in stark contrast to their lagging efforts to help the self-employed, the unemployed and the asset-poor. The long-term effects of this crisis and the state response to it are not yet clear. But if, as seems likely, the next several years witness a significant increase in market concentration as weaker firms are swallowed up by smaller ones, along with a dramatic expansion in the size of the state, we could be entering a new era of state-monopoly capitalism, under which the interests of senior politicians, financiers and corporate executives become fused into one.

How should socialists orient themselves in this age of upheaval? We have to consolidate a new popular mood of mutuality and solidarity, argues Sam Gindin, and get ourselves off the back foot. 'This is a moment to think more ambitiously,' he insists. There is widespread agreement among our contributors that while the left eventually found positive expression in the multiple insurgent political movements that emerged in a variety of national contexts, it failed to respond constructively to the potential energy released by the last crisis, the financial meltdown of 2008. Our collective assumption that the sub-prime crisis – the panic that it spread throughout the financial system and the consequent collapse of the global economy – would confirm all the socialist adages about the inherent unsustainability of capitalism proved hopelessly naïve. Our initial failure to translate the widespread dissatisfaction with the economic and political consensus that followed into a progressive movement for change led to the subjugation of countless millions across the world under brutal austerity regimes. Perhaps the slowness of our response, given the depths into which the movement had sunk, was to be expected. But we cannot afford to make the same mistakes again.

This book seeks, as far as is possible, to make sense of the astonishing political moment in which we find ourselves – beginning with the financial crisis of 2008 and ending with the coronavirus crisis of 2020 – and chart a course forward. Much as Anthony Crosland's *The Future of Socialism* acted as a touchstone for liberals within the Labour Party over the course of the mid- to late twentieth century, we hope that this book will lay out the beginnings of a strategy for socialists to pursue, both within and outside the Labour Party, for years to come.

In the wake of 2019, commentators from across the political spectrum were quick to pronounce the final collapse of class politics. When measured according to the income and occupation-based class metrics developed in the mid- to late twentieth century, this picture checks out. The Conservatives performed better among lower-middle- and working-class (C2DE)voters in the 2019 election than it did among middle- and upper-class voters (ABC1), based on the UK's National Statistical Socio-Economic Classification (NS-SEC) schema. But such schemas completely fail to capture the transformations that have taken place in the class structure of British society since the financial crisis.

In his contribution to this collection, Keir Milburn questions this narrative by arguing that the real story of the last two general elections has been not the declining importance of class, but the growing salience of age – a divide which has a solid material basis. The generational divide that now marks electoral politics across the rich world results from the austere legacy of the pre-crisis boom: the material interests of older home-owners nearing the end of their working lives, the core of the Conservative electoral coalition, 'are currently tied to the value of residential real estate and, because their pensions are invested in stock markets, the performance of the financial sector'. The interests of younger voters, generally on low wages, in insecure work and living in the private rented sector, are diametrically opposed to those of their forebears. Generation Left, argues Milburn, comprises those who have come of age in the wreckage of the economic model that enriched their parents; they have no real interest in continuing to support the status quo. Now facing another deep economic crisis, will today's young people grow into a politics of reaction, or retain their socialistic instincts?

Another much remarked-upon aspect of the 2019 election was the astonishing geographical distribution of votes. Labour lost seats across English regions that it had held for decades, as the 'Red Wall' finally crumbled. One did not have to look far to find members of the commentariat arguing that Jeremy Corbyn bore responsibility for severing the longstanding bond between the Labour Party and working-class voters in the North of England. As Tom Hazeldine shows in this volume, this claim is misleading: Labour's declining popularity in the North is part of a gradual trend that dates back to the Blair years. Hazeldine interrogates opposing claims that the left must either resist this trend or ride it, by focusing its energies on building support among progressive liberal voters within England's cities and the burgeoning working class in many southern towns.

The answer will, in no small part, be determined by Johnson's ability to hold together his new electoral coalition. In his first Budget speech, Johnson's newly anointed Chancellor, Rishi

Sunak, announced he would be releasing a wave of investment for the North and the Midlands; but even before the world was plunged into a renewed global economic crisis, replacing their outdated rail systems seemed unlikely to provide England's regions with enough productive heft to counter the extraordinary weight of a first city engorged on capital sucked in from every corner of the globe. If northern voters really did 'lend' Johnson their votes, he will need to pull many more policies out of Labour's playbook to hold on to them over the long haul. Whether or not the rest of his party – and indeed British capital – will allow him to do so remains an open question.

Owen Hatherley reflects on the longstanding parting of ways between the Labour Party and older voters in England's northern regions, through the eyes of one of the North's best loved bands, The Smiths. Morrissey's trajectory, from apparently anti-establishment, working-class origins to the reactionary xenophobia of his later years, argues Hatherley, reflects similar journeys undertaken by many children of Margaret Thatcher's Britain. In his vivid contribution, Hatherley explores what the music of The Smiths, and the political unravelling of its lead singer, can tell us about the English character. The way in which Morrissey at once despises and idealises the pain of his childhood reflects 'the nostalgia for misery, a longing for boredom, a relocation of poverty from economics to aesthetics' of the older middle-class voters who delivered the Conservatives their victory.

Meanwhile, in Scotland, Labour was once again routed by the Scottish National Party (SNP). The Party now holds just one seat in Scotland, next to six for the Conservatives, four for the Liberal Democrats and forty-eight for the Scottish National Party. The SNP's success, Rory Scothorne argues in this volume, has rested on its ability to portray itself as a traditional social-democratic party of the kind you would expect to find in a typical small north European state. Yet as the party has consolidated its hegemony in Scotland, its leaders have 'diluted this left-leaning identity'. Can Labour recover its electoral fortunes in Scotland simply by attempting to outflank the SNP from the left, as seems to have been Corbyn's strategy? As Scothorne argues, it is only by confronting the question of independence head on that the Party can hope to rebuild its battered reputation in Scotland.

The Labour Party's ambivalence over constitutional questions extends beyond Scottish independence to the issue that dominated the 2019 general election in England, Wales and Northern Ireland: Brexit. Andrew Murray places the blame for Labour's defeat squarely on the shoulders of those who pushed the Party towards campaigning for a second referendum on Britain's membership of the European Union. But the mistakes made by the Labour Party could not simply be attributed to electoral miscalculation: they were symptomatic of a deeper ideological confusion between socialism and liberalism, which has contributed to defeats experienced by socialist parties across the bloc. Murray considers how, as the legitimacy of the liberal establishment has been steadily eroded, the right has made hay from the European question, developing a critique of the bloc that blends a rejection of the enforcement of neoliberal policies with a xenophobic, nationalistic reaction to the erosion of the imperial power of the once-dominant British nation state. His contribution explores how Johnson successfully passed himself off as a left-populist, 'wielding nation-state power to protect the economic interests of the people' while Labour was perceived as 'belonging to a stonewalling establishment'.

It seems unlikely that, had the Party maintained its 2019 commitment to respecting the result of the referendum, it would have lost more votes to the Liberal Democrats – and indeed that those lost votes would translate into such a staggering loss of seats – than it did to the Conservatives. Even so, with the right completely united after the Conservative–Brexit Party pact, and half the country united behind them, it also seems unlikely that a weak pro-Leave message would have saved Labour from defeat. And after the rout of the local elections, the internal struggle faced by the leadership in entering another election with the same position would have been phenomenal. Not only the Parliamentary Labour Party, but members too, would likely have revolted – indeed, Murray concedes that by 2019 the leadership faced few other options. In the era of the culture war, socialist parties face few good options: give up on class politics altogether and take up arms alongside progressive liberals, or hope to drown out the politics of reaction with a populist economic message.

Jeremy Gilbert cautions against such binary political thinking: if the Labour Party is to succeed in winning state power on a platform that includes socialist elements, it must build out its electoral coalition 'in all directions'. The return of the socialist left from the depths of the 1990s defeats, when the apparent 'end of history' seemed to signal the death of the left as a coherent political force, is, argues Gilbert, quite astonishing – even as it represents a reversion to 'normal' historical conditions. The successes of the *new* new left are evident from the extent to which these movements have transformed the dominant economic 'common sense' – now evident in the generous responses by right-wing governments to the crisis consuming the global economy. But even these successes do not negate the lesson the Party should have learned from historical experience: the UK media landscape is irreconcilably hostile and our majoritarian electoral system offers the Conservatives, with their efficient, geographically dispersed voter base, a permanent upper hand. Gilbert explores the options for socialist strategy in light of these constraints, weighing up the arguments for and against fighting to broaden the progressive electoral coalition by championing electoral reform and cooperating with other parties where possible in the meantime.

The feature that differentiates the Labour Party from other potential members of a progressive coalition is that it emerged as the vehicle for the electoral representation of the trade union movement and retains a close link with the labour movement. But Dalia Gebrial highlights how the changing composition of the labour force – in particular, the rise of precarious employment and underemployment – poses challenges to both the labour movement and the Labour Party. The strategies employed by capital to undermine the once-stable categories of 'work', 'worker' and 'workplace', inflected with gendered and racialised logics, have both supported accumulation since the crisis of 2008 and further fractured an already divided workforce. As the right seeks to exploit these divisions in service of their culture war between the 'metropolitan elite' and the 'traditional working class', socialists must rethink the strategies they use to organise and mobilise working people. Gebrial argues that the principle of 'universal access to the means of life' must be a central feature of socialist strategy in the age of precarity.

The question posed by Gargi Bhattacharyya is how the left might acquire some new habits to allow us collectively to imagine a new world, one based on 'mutuality, survival and justice'. The left's focus on electoralism, while important, has taken precedence over the centring of the lived experience of the British working classes – many of whom are simply struggling to survive from one day to the next. Bhattacharyya's essay challenges socialists to look at strategy with new eyes – not those of a movement triumphantly marching towards victory, understood as the capture of the state, but those of communities working together to build a better world from the ground up without diverting too much energy from the daily pressures of survival. Our movement must be as deeply aware of our mutual interdependence in the working class's struggle for survival and recovery as it is of the traditional hallmarks of strategy: the state, the economy and the media. Bhattacharyya does, however, recognise that 'the continuous onslaught of character assassination and outright lies [by the UK media] shaped the extent of the Labour defeat'. This onslaught and character assassination are the subject of Tom Mills's essay on the relationship between the Labour Party and the UK media.

Mills argues that socialists have too often ignored the constraints imposed upon the Labour Party in general, and socialists within the Labour Party in particular, by the UK's hostile media. Over the last several decades, and particularly during the Thatcherite assault on the UK's public institutions, both the print and broadcast media – including the BBC – became steadily more hostile to Labour. Blair's conciliation with the media, effected by providing Britain's media barons with a veto over Labour Party policy, was the exception that proved the rule. How, then, can socialists hope to organise in the context of such a powerful coalition of forces ranged against them? Mills explores the case both for the construction of an expansive left media infrastructure, and for developing policy that could be used to transform the UK's media landscape once Labour is in power.

The electoral defeat of a socialist-led Labour Party by a Conservative Party united around a politics of nationalist reaction and spurred on by the right-wing press has one obvious historical parallel: the election of 1983, when a Labour Party led by Michael Foot on a socialist platform was pummelled by Thatcher's Conservatives, even as unemployment hit the 3 million mark in 1982. Rory MacQueen interrogates the comparison between 1983 and 2019 with reference to a post-election pamphlet not dissimilar to this one, *The Future of the Left*. Grappling with Labour's electoral defeat, Tony Benn mused: 'If hope is to replace fear, people have to be able to believe that there is an alternative. Unfortunately for us, the electorate did not believe in Labour's alternative – and wondered whether we all believed in it either.' MacQueen points to the relevance of these lessons for today's Labour Party: Thatcher's resounding success at communicating an 'alternative way of life' stood in stark contrast to Labour's inability to provide a picture of what life would really be like under socialism. Unable to sketch the contours of a new political horizon, the construction of a progressive alliance based around support for the continuation of the Keynesian politics of the post-war consensus would not, argued Raymond Williams in *The Future of the Left*, deliver renewed electoral success for Labour. MacQueen analyses the ongoing relevance of the arguments made by Benn, Williams and others in the wake of another defeat for the left, cautioning that the main lesson the Labour left must learn from history is that only a party united around its own manifesto will ever be capable of winning elections.

The question of Party unity is, argues Leo Panitch, central to the question of the left's electoral failure; but with most Labour members united behind the establishment-endorsed leader Sir Keir Starmer, will Party unity now be used as a bat to beat back socialist policies? In an interview with the editor, Panitch considers a reversion to Blairism under Starmer's leadership unlikely. However, he predicts that the direction of travel – at least at the top of the Party – will be towards an equivocal 'politics of compromise', cautioning that, with the Conservatives united, such a move will only create 'ideological confusion' among the majority of the membership. How to prevent confusion, disorganisation and conflict from emerging within the left? Panitch gestures to the critical importance of political education. How might socialists turn CLPs into 'interesting centres of working-class life'? And how might they organise to change the nature of union branches? Only once these things are achieved can socialists hope to take charge of the party apparatus, and build unity around a new, socialist common sense.

This process, argues James Schneider, will not be a swift one. In many ways, the defining feature of the Corbyn project was its unique ability to 'occupy the gap' left by the absence of progressive forces in the UK. The decline of the labour movement has been, perhaps, the most obvious manifestation of this absence; but the defanging of local government, the steady erosion of cultural centres of working-class life and the failure of the loose constellation of social movements on the left to coalesce into a more organised bloc were also factors. In 2016, what remained of the UK's progressive social forces flocked into the Labour Party to support Jeremy Corbyn; Schneider offers an insider's perspective on the challenge of transforming this group of progressively minded individuals into an organised entity capable of engaging in a process of class formation. The huge successes achieved over the last four years were, he argues, largely driven by the contingent fact that Corbyn's coalition never really shifted out of campaign mode, which forced those who believed in the project to subdue their differences for longer than might otherwise have been the case. In the wake of the 2019 defeat, Schneider considers the implications of the social forces that underpinned

Corbynism splitting off in a variety of different directions. While this process of separation may prove messy, argues Schneider, it 'need not be disastrously divisive and is, indeed, necessary'.

How might socialists use this period of reconstruction to bridge another gap – that which separates the United Kingdom from the United States? Joe Guinan and Sarah McKinley reflect on the fortunes of the transatlantic left – the increasingly unified socialist movement that has emerged around the prime ministerial and presidential campaigns of Jeremy Corbyn and Bernie Sanders respectively. Schneider and Panitch argue that the electoral focus of both movements involved an attempt to find a shortcut around the longer-term process of movement building. Guinan and McKinley assess how socialists in the US and the UK can work together to learn the lessons of their respective defeat, and build a stronger, more cohesive and more strategic socialist movement. The foundations of this project have already been laid in the form of the complementary policy programmes developed by both projects, but Guinan and McKinley reflect on the need to develop a much deeper level of cooperation, one that prioritises genuine solidarity, mutual care and long-term resilience.

If social movements and political parties must cooperate in the post-Corbyn era, how should each orient itself? Just one month after Corbyn's defeat, points out Cristina Flesher Fominaya, Unidas Podemos – the radical socialist party founded in the wake of the post-crisis 15M protest movement – entered a coalition government with the Spanish centre-left PSOE (Partido Socialista Obrero Español or the Spanish Socialist Workers' Party). Podemos, argues Fominaya, has channelled 'widespread dissatisfaction with established politics' into electoral success, where in other contexts this strategy has been the preserve of the right. What lessons can movement parties – which seek to retain characteristics of social movements while attempting to acquire executive power – such as Podemos provide for socialists in other national contexts? The answer to this question, argues Fominaya, hinges on the balance these parties strike between 'real democracy' and the imperatives of electoral politics. She analyses the challenges of effecting this balance within Podemos, which now seems to resemble a hollowed-out 'classical party' more than a socially embedded 'challenger movement'. Nevertheless, the movement parties in Europe's western periphery – in Spain, Portugal and Ireland – now appear stronger than those in the US and the UK. Socialists everywhere will be watching very closely for clues as to how the challenges posed by movement parties can be resolved.

In his contribution, Chris Saltmarsh explores the claim that the timeline of the impending climate crisis militates against such long-term socialist strategising, and instead lends itself to the agile politics of protest that have dominated the environmentalist movement for decades. Many members of environmentalist groups such as Extinction Rebellion have taken Labour's defeat at the polls as a vindication of their anti-political, anti-statist stance. As the economic collapse resulting from the world's response to the coronavirus pandemic has sent carbon emissions tumbling, some members of these groups are now veering towards an eco-fascism that sees the hundreds of thousands of deaths likely to result from the virus as a necessary correction to humanity's dominance over the earth. Saltmarsh warns against anti-electoral reaction among the climate movement, arguing that the time-frame of climate breakdown requires eco-socialists to buttress a continuing orientation towards electoral politics with a commitment to 'building a more diverse power base from below'. He interrogates the strategic options both for eco-socialists seeking to organise within the Labour Party, and for those engaging in new forms of political struggle within the labour movement and local communities.

But the global South is where the ecological crisis is presenting itself most acutely. The focus of the contribution from Vijay Prashad, Richard Pithouse and P. Sainath is on the way in which climate breakdown and COVID-19 are exacerbating the inadequacies of our existing food production and distribution systems, with dire consequences for the poorest people on the planet. Acute hunger is, just like climate breakdown, disproportionately likely to affect the 'dispossessed' – those who have been expelled from their land and denied access to the basic means of subsistence. Under capitalism, food is a commodity – not a human right – and under hyper-globalised, financialised capitalism, agricultural production has become 'enveloped into a global supply chain'. Farmers in the global South receive a tiny portion of the value of the commodity they produce, while speculators in the City of London generate huge returns from bets made on commodity prices, which in turn influence the terms of trade for some of the poorest countries on the planet. The irrationality – and inhumanity – of this system has been starkly exposed by the coronavirus pandemic. In response, the authors demand a radical restructuring of global food production and distribution based on 'popular control over the food system'.

The global inequities of power and wealth generated by an imperialistic world system are not only evident in agriculture. Ashok Kumar's essay focuses on the struggles of textile workers in Bangladesh against the extractive global supply chains that mark the garment industry. Kumar shows how the pandemic is shifting the terrain on which this battle is fought. Monopoly and monopsony power are central to Kumar's analysis – the monopolistic brands with which many consumers in the West are familiar are also international monopsonies, some of the largest purchasers in their respective markets. In the textiles sector, this has historically created significant asymmetries of power between buyers and sellers, further entrenching the imperialistic relationships between global North and South. Kumar interrogates how these relationships are shifting in the context of the pandemic – particularly given its dramatic impact on global supply chains – and how these shifts are affecting the organising strategies of some of the most marginalised workers in the world.

Sita Balani's contribution reflects on the impact of the pandemic on workers in the United Kingdom, who spend each day living with the intimate knowledge of death. Balani reminds us that 'knowledge alone is not power' – just because we know that our government's actions have contributed to the deaths of thousands, this does not make us any more able to stop them. In a country where our prime minister has progressed from attempting to downplay the severity of the virus to simply disappearing from view; where our media seem to lack 'any desire to seek the truth'; and where politicians seem to get away with treating citizens with a thinly veiled contempt, it would be easy to lapse into a state of despair given the severity of the challenges we face. Balani's piece looks past the triumphalism of those who seek to 'use' this moment to implement radical, top-down policy solutions, and into the springs of optimism arising from the emergence of mutual support networks, through which people have learned to live in a world created by the ruling classes, while also defying its authoritarian logic.

Over the past decade, working people across the UK have organised to defy the brutal austerity regime imposed by the Conservatives in the wake of the financial crisis. Siân Errington reflects on how this fight will continue in the context of a pandemic that has seen government spending increase substantially.

The result of Tory austerity was as economically senseless as it has been morally tragic: the UK has endured a near unprecedented decade of stagnation, in incomes, productivity and investment. With a new economic crisis now rippling throughout the global economy, the right is teaching the left a new lesson in the politics of the shock doctrine: there is no limit to the amount governments will spend in order to save capitalism. As public spending increases, some on the left are claiming victory in the battle of ideas, but Errington cautions against this statist reading of anti-austerity politics: Corbyn's leadership was about more than simply standing against the cuts: 'it represented a new vision of how the government should intervene in the economy and society.'

Why, then, has it been so easy for so many to conclude that the Corbyn project was about little more than advocating for a slight increase in public spending? James Meadway's contribution grapples with this question, arguing that, over the course of Corbyn's leadership, the project's insurgent character was muted as questions of policy detail replaced those of socialist strategy. The 2019 manifesto was simultaneously ambitious in its scope and modest in its ambition: the level of detail was impressive, but the sum of policies such as the Green New Deal, the creation of a National Investment Bank and investment in public services amounted, in the end, simply to a reheating of the Keynesian politics of the post-war period. Nowhere is this clearer than in the Party's strategy for challenging the dominance of the finance sector in British political economy: where the 2017 manifesto contained some fairly radical proposals for transforming the finance sector, the 2019 manifesto simply mused on the mechanics of constructing a public banking system. Meadway interrogates how socialists can recover both their insurgent character and their sweeping strategic orientation, while resisting the authoritarian tendencies unleashed by the Conservative response to the coronavirus crisis. He calls for centring the question of democracy in both policy development and organising.

Cat Hobbs, who has been campaigning on the issue of public ownership for many years, explores how socialists might achieve such a democratic reorientation. Hobbs charts the dramatic increase in support for public ownership witnessed over the last several years, laying out in detail the arguments she and fellow campaigners have honed in support of collective ownership of our most important national assets. The left's success in building a new consensus in favour of public ownership has proven timely for the Conservatives, who will likely be forced to take significant public stakes in many large corporations as the coronavirus crisis worsens. Hobbs explores the conditions that socialists must insist upon regarding the use of public money for corporate bailouts, 'so these bailouts do not serve simply to enrich private shareholders at the expense of people and planet'. Over the longer term, she lays out a democratic socialist vision for recovery from the crisis, centred on public democratic ownership of key infrastructure and a Green New Deal aimed at reflating, and decarbonising, our battered economy.

The coronavirus has not simply highlighted the unsustainability of our economic model, argues Daniel Gerke; it has contributed to the erosion of the ideology of capitalist realism, increasingly under threat ever since the financial crisis of 2008. Socialist culture in such an age must, he believes, be structured around a 'radical political realism', which emphasises modernism, humanism and realism – in contrast both to the nostalgia and anti-humanism of the right, and to the anti-materialism of postmodernists. The left must acknowledge the power of capitalist realism, the remnants of which undoubtedly contributed to the Labour Party's 2019 defeat, and the real constraints imposed on human beings by the imperatives of capital accumulation, while emphasising the possibility of constructing a new politics and encouraging collective attempts to imagine and build it. Gerke explores how the shifts currently being generated by the coronavirus pandemic might reinforce the message that we are constantly engaged in a process of constructing political, economic and cultural consensus, and how socialists can fight to ensure this process is progressive in nature.

As well as exposing cracks in the edifice of capitalist realism, the coronavirus crisis has revealed the fundamentally human basis of our economy. The renewed appreciation of what has traditionally been seen as 'women's work' – nursing and care work, for example – has come as no surprise to feminist writers who have been documenting the marginalisation of workers in these sectors for decades. This new appreciation for social reproduction could form the basis for what Amelia Horgan calls 'socialist feminism': 'a feminism that takes issues of class, work and the relationship between production and reproduction seriously'. Horgan explores the ways in which the arguments made by socialist feminists have been obscured by the dominant strands of capitalist-friendly feminism, which she divides into corporate feminism and what she terms the 'personal brand feminism'. Both are based on a liberal, individualistic account of politics and society, but are also built on the lessons of radical feminism – specifically, the idea that there are 'distinct female ways of being'. How might a socialist feminist revival fostered by this crisis – based on an acceptance of the centrality of social reproduction in production, without naturalising it as an inherently 'feminine' activity – be undercut by the tendency of liberal feminism to mystify and idealise care work, without recognising its often exploitative and oppressive character?

As this book went to press, anti-racism protests catalysed by the murder of George Floyd by US police were rippling across the UK; Joshua Virasami and Simukai Chigudu reflect on the openings the protests have created and the challenges they pose for the British left. Virasami exhorts those who see themselves as allies of the Black Lives Matter movement to take action in support of the protestors: 'to be anti-racist means to involve yourself directly in the movement to end racism, to take action'. He interrogates the way in which racism is woven into the structures of a global economy reproduced only through the poorly paid labour of the dispossessed, under the constant threat of violence and imperialist war. Any action aimed at challenging racism must also take aim at the structures upon which it is built: anti-racism is anti-capitalism, and vice versa. Virasami explores how members of the socialist movement might undertake the transition from 'passive non-racist' to 'active anti-racist', emphasising how much we have to learn from those socialist anti-racists who came before us.

Simukai Chigudu writes of his own journey as a Zimbabwean academic and anti-racist campaigner, from his participation in the Rhodes Must Fall (RMF) movement that began in 2015, through to the toppling of the statue of Edward Colston in Bristol in 2020. Chigudu, one of just seven black professors at Oxford, remembers the 'hostile, infantilising and casually racist' responses of journalists and commentators to the RMF movement in 2015. He reflects on hearing high-profile white academics accuse students like him of attempting to erase history. In fact, movements like RMF and the recent Black Lives Matter protests have created the only moments when activists have been able to start honest conversations about the legacy of British colonialism and racism in the UK. Racism in the UK will not end with the toppling of a statue – the hard work of anti-racist activists will continue. The future of socialism depends on this struggle.

Entering the 2020s and surveying the prospects of the movement that has, for these last few years, dominated the horizons of our lives, it would be easy for this book's contributors to allow themselves more than a hint of despondency, or even despair. What is remarkable about the essays collected here is the thread of optimism that winds its way through them all. Are we naïve to hope things will turn out any differently this time? Perhaps, not least because we are now entering what is likely to be one of the most challenging decades in recent history; but it would also be unrealistically cynical to suggest that there are not grounds for optimism. Lola Seaton's contribution to this book seems to reflect the experiences of new activists across the country, in that the anguish of defeat has not dented her determination to continue fighting for a better world.

Editing these pieces while in lockdown, surrounded by apocalyptic stories of the unfolding pandemic, I felt this optimism quite deeply. It is not a hope driven by an objective assessment of the forces mounted against the socialist movement; nor is it a hope driven by the internal contradictions of the capitalist system, which, if anything, seem to have proved more help to the reactionary right than the socialist left. It is a hope driven by my admiration for the wisdom, strength and immense compassion of my friends and comrades on the left, many of whom have contributed to this collection. If we can learn anything from the crisis currently engulfing the planet, it is that we survive individually only through our strength as a collective – this lesson applies to political movements as much as to communities or societies. When I reflect on the solidarity that continues to exist between those engaged in the struggle to build a better world, in spite of all our setbacks and defeats, it seems that we cannot help but survive this era of crisis – and that we may even learn to thrive.

I. FOUNDATIONS

1

A New North?

Tom Hazeldine

Politics makes strange bedfellows, but few as strange as these. On 12 December 2019 (it seems a long time ago now), a Conservative prime minister and former London mayor of broadly Thatcherite cast sealed a rapprochement with the towns and pit communities eviscerated by the neoliberal restructuring of the Thatcher, Major and Blair years. Boris Johnson is praiseful of Thatcher's legacy, 'whose benefits we enjoy to this day', but he has succeeded where Conservatives of her generation feared to tread.[*] He won twenty-eight northern and sixteen Midland constituencies from Labour: forty-four seats in total, out of a national net gain of forty-eight. As a result, one in five Conservative MPs represents a northern constituency, the highest proportion in half a century. Without these regional additions, Johnson would have a working Commons majority of minus one.

---

[*] Boris Johnson, 'What Would Maggie Do Today?', speech at the Centre for Policy Studies, 27 November 2013. See also Emma Duncan, 'The New North', *Sunday Times*, 6 May 1990, a defence of Thatcher's regional record.

It was Labour's blocking of EU withdrawal that precipitated a general election in which the Party inevitably leaked support on both flanks, to the pro-Brexit Conservatives and hard-Remain Lib Dems. But the concentration of Labour losses gains in Leave-voting, working-class areas of the North was overwhelming. Constituents in Ashton-under-Lyne on the outskirts of Manchester were 'more despondent than in 2017', Angela Rayner told the *Guardian* ahead of the poll. 'They wanted one thing done and it's not happened – and they hate us all'. Two years earlier, when Corbyn had pledged to respect the referendum decision while seeking a close relationship with the EU-27, he boosted the Party's vote share in the North by 10 percentage points. In 2019 it dropped by the same margin. Although the Tony Blair Institute accuses Corbyn's leadership and politics of causing a 'rupture with long-held loyalties', the Party's malaise in its heartlands is more deeply rooted. Even in defeat, Corbyn polled more votes in the region than New Labour, once in power, ever attracted.

Two types of response to the loss of 'Red Wall' constituencies emerged on the Labour left. 'Why should Labour's support be eternally in the North?' pondered Richard Seymour in *Salvage*:

> Suppose the new working class, less organised than its forebear, expands outside of these former heartland towns? Suppose the left's purchase is indeed found in new parts of the South? If so, isn't that a trend we just have to get ahead of?

Alternatively, Craig Gent of Novara argued for the scaling up of community organising in coalfield seats 'not out of calculation but because it's the right thing to do. Only then will people start "coming home" to Labour.'

---

* Richard Seymour, 'Losing the North', *Salvage*, 26 January 2020; Craig Gent, 'Learning the Lessons of Labour's Northern Nightmare Will Take Longer Than a Weekend', Novara, 17 December 2019.

These reflections came before Keir Starmer's election as Labour leader. 'Britain now has someone at the forefront of public life who has, throughout his career, inclined toward caution and the status quo,' celebrates the *Spectator*.* The problem with Gent's proposal, therefore, is that by continuing to work through the Labour Party, former Corbynistas may expend a lot of effort just to function as foot soldiers for a hard-boiled pro-capitalist, pro-NATO party leadership.

For socialists to abandon the deindustrialised English rustbelt wholesale, on the other hand, would be to cede a lot of ground to the neoliberals and risk political headwinds from these quarters, such as the pro-Leave sentiment that sank Corbyn in 2019. National hegemony can't be mustered from the cities alone, and the average southern town – not the likes of hippy Stroud – has its share of political-cultural reaction. Owen Hatherley suggests in *Tribune* that English culture is defined by its nastiness, and the emotional temperature is noticeably cooler in southern parts.

Northern England and the Midlands are predominantly working-class societies; southern England is not. At the last census, the C2DE social grades (manual workers, casual workers, the unemployed) made up 52 per cent of the population in the North and 51 per cent in the Midlands compared to 38 per cent in London and 43 per cent in the rest of the South. It would still be possible to pursue the Bennite objective of 'a fundamental and irreversible shift in the balance of wealth and power in favour of working people' by organising in the latter regions, one should expect the politics of the salariat to loom larger.

---

* 'Given a choice between the new and unknown and the familiar and safe, he has always opted for the latter': David Patrikarakos, 'Keir Starmer Is the Conservative We Need in this Time of Crisis', *Spectator*, 15 April 2020. Cf. Oliver Eagleton, 'What Keir Starmer's Ambition of "Unity" Really Means', Novara, 4 April 2020.

Will Johnson's electoral coalition hold? Presentationally, the prime minister got off to a good start: a Brexit-day meeting of the Cabinet in Sunderland; nationalisation of the hopeless Northern Rail; plans for a Treasury 'economic decision-making campus' in the region, possibly on Teesside; talk of moving the House of Lords to York, and of creating a second Conservative Party headquarters in the North or Midlands (somewhere 'well placed in political terms', according to ConservativeHome). Johnson followed up a post-election visit to Sedgefield with the offer of £70 million towards conversion of the former Redcar steelworks – sold off by Thatcher in 1988 and shuttered by Thai multinational SSI under Cameron in 2015 – into a private-sector business park. Redcar had become Bluecar, the prime minister joked with his aides: it needed to be looked after. Atop all this, there is his pledge to 'level up' a country with some of the worst regional disparities in the advanced capitalist world.

Every Westminster government promises something of the sort. How should Johnson's commitment be assessed, and is it made more or less plausible in light of the 2020 crash?

Few writers discuss the North–South divide for long without reaching for Orwell. Let's leave *The Road to Wigan Pier* to one side, for a change, and consult *Down and Out in Paris and London* instead. I'm thinking of his pungent description of life in the grand 'Hôtel X.' near the Place de la Concorde, and the contrast he draws between the waiters' outward show of polished manners and their slovenly behaviour in the kitchens. There is a fatal tension in the whole business of fine dining, Orwell argues:

> In a hotel a huge and complicated machine is kept running by an inadequate staff, because every man has a well-defined job and does it scrupulously. But there is a weak point, and it is this – that the job the staff are doing is not necessarily what the customer pays for.

The customer pays, as he sees it, for good service; the employee is paid, as he sees it, for the *boulot* – meaning, as a rule, an imitation of good service.

This is what UK regional policy has always previously amounted to: an imitation of good service, to avoid political embarrassment from worsening economic disparities. 'It is not a question of spending a great deal of money, but of showing that the matter has not been pigeon-holed, and that the government is doing its best to help matters', Neville Chamberlain told the National Government in 1934; or, as Chancellor Derick Heathcoat-Amory advised Harold Macmillan in 1958, 'We must take all the action we reasonably can to deal with this problem; and, equally important, we must be seen to be doing so.'

The same dynamic has played out time and again, because the country's spatial hierarchies – the City of London at the summit, the South-East stockbroker belt just below it, outlying industrial or post-industrial regions bottommost – have only become more entrenched as the years pass. Harold Wilson ramped up spending on regional industrial subsidies to deflect criticism over colliery closures and the collapse of his National Plan under financial market pressure. Thatcher forced a shakeout among domestic manufacturers while renovating the Square Mile, but confessed grudging admiration for Michael Heseltine's 'skilful public relations' in showing an interest in recession-ravaged Merseyside after the Toxteth riots.

Blair assured the *Northern Echo* and his County Durham constituents that 'there is a North–South divide' and 'we do have to bridge it'. At the same time, he and Brown defended the Bank of England's policy to raise interest rates to dampen inflationary pressure in the South East, no matter if its effect on the currency exchanges was to price industrial exporters out of world markets. Blair's chief press secretary orchestrated national headlines stating that the regional gap was in fact 'over', 'dead' and a 'myth'. Cameron and Osborne protested that the UK was too London-centric, then proceeded to inflate another asset price bubble in the City through quantitative easing, while towns such as Blackpool bore the brunt of austerity.

So what's new? Writing in *New Left Review* in 2016, William Davies sketched out three ethical–historical phases of neoliberalism: the combative Thatcherite and Reaganite variety of 1979–89; the uncontested normative neoliberalism of 1989–2008; and the punitive type of recent years, organised around austerity and benefit sanctions. The coming to power of Johnson and Cummings in summer 2019 may have signalled a local shift to a more populist iteration. Davies thought not, dismissing the pair in the *Guardian* as ideological bankrupts with nothing but Brexit in the locker. But it's arguable that they represent one of neoliberalism's more creative rearguard responses to the travails of the post-2008 period. Their back-to-back victories in the Brexit referendum and 2019 general election came through a willingness to trade in the four freedoms of the EU single market – unhindered cross-border movement of goods, capital, services and persons – for an electoral compact with the UK's left-behind regions, one that kept Corbynism at bay while protecting market imperatives within the national economic arena.

Before the coronavirus struck, Conservative regional policy continued to place a New Labour-ish emphasis on supply-side improvements: skills training, infrastructure investment. Chancellor Rishi Sunak – a former City hedge fund manager and MP for the picturesque castle town of Richmond in the Yorkshire Dales – set aside large sums for capital spending in his March 2020 Budget. He also confirmed that the assessment criteria of the Green Book (used by the Treasury to calculate return on investment for public infrastructure), which tilts transport investment towards London and the South East, were to be reviewed. Any loosening of the purse-strings would help regional economies damaged by the spending cuts of 2010–19. Services account for 76 per cent of economic output in the North and public services are easily the largest subsector. The planned increases in current expenditure were fairly modest – some of the sums involved merely replace EU funding – but it's fair to say that the pre-Covid Johnson administration combined an intent to dish Labour through higher day-to-day spending with a commitment to 'boosterism' on the capital account.

The timing of the Budget caught Sunak torn between the election pledges of 2019 and a worsening public health emergency. Every judgement is provisional in the wake of the pandemic. However, either London or the South East has bounced back strongest from every national recession since at least the 1973 OPEC price shock, and there is no ipso facto reason to suppose things will be different this time. The North West posted the largest initial rise in the unemployment claimant rate during the spring 2020 lockdown, while the steepest expected falls in GDP in the second quarter of the year were in northern and Midland areas especially reliant on lockdown-prone sectors – manufacturing, for example, in the case of Corby, Pendle and the Ribble Valley. Financial and insurance services in the City of London and Edinburgh were forecast to weather the economic storm better (as were deprived areas with large health and social work sectors, from Middlesbrough to Tower Hamlets).

Over the longer term, the corona-related drag on economic activity will impair balance sheets in all institutional sectors of the economy. The Treasury accepts that central government

debt-to-GDP levels must rise but urges a fiscal consolidation to
plug a forecast annual budget deficit of £340bn, twice the gap
that opened up after the financial crisis. In the corporate world,
any repeat of the regionalised credit crunch of 2008–10, when
the UK's centralised banking system rebalanced loan portfolios
to favour firms closest to headquarters, will hurt northern and
Midland SMEs more than their southern counterparts. Among
households, whereas median debt excluding mortgages doesn't
vary widely between regions, median net property wealth rose
by 51 per cent in London in the post-2008 decade to £410,000
while falling 12 per cent in the North East to £115,000. Another
round of quantitative easing – including £200bn from the Bank
of England, equivalent to 9 per cent of GDP – has partially
corrected the slump in equity prices of February–March 2020,
important for London in particular where financial wealth makes
an unusually large contribution to overall household wealth.

The contraction of global capitalist supply chains now
predicted by David Harvey among others could create opportunities for producers in rustbelt regions in the West.[*] The
prime minister's senior advisor, Dominic Cummings, is bent on
overhauling the state bureaucracy – as he writes on his blog,
'changing the wiring of power in Whitehall so decisions are
better'. He also has at least a hobby-horse interest in private
sector technological innovation, modelled on Californian prec-
edents. Raised in Durham, like Blair, and retaining more of an
accent, might he foster a programme of industrial–scientific
modernisation in his home region? It seems unlikely. Awed reverence for market rationality won't dispose him to intervene in
firms' locational decisions. Only electoral motives would cause

---

[*]   David Harvey, 'Anti-Capitalist Politics in the Time of COVID-19',
Jacobin, 20 March 2020.

the government to send corporate R&D support further north than, say, Cheltenham and Cambridge. But then, such motives are real forces.

If COVID-19 forced a general shift to massive state intervention across the OECD, it became clear as national lockdowns eased that neoliberalism in one form or another had merely been suspended, pending a return, when market relations could once more dictate social life. In those UK regions stranded by the market, grievances will extend beyond the millennial and post-millennial precariat that powers the post-Corbyn left to also include many of Johnson's small-town voters; as dismayed as anyone by the government's mishandling of the crisis, they expected good service from the Conservatives and have no party loyalties to cause them to settle for less. Any socialist movement worth its salt would marry up these malcontents.

2

The Experience of Defeat

Lola Seaton

I was very late to the Corbyn Party. Like many of my peers, I had never canvassed before the 2019 election, and I started doing so for a Party of which I wasn't even yet a member (I rejoined so recently I wasn't eligible to attend my Constituency Labour Party's nomination meeting), and for which I'd felt only the barest, most grudging electoral loyalty prior to 2015. My support for previous incarnations of the Labour Party had been so nominal and half-hearted that it had never occurred to me to spend time persuading others to vote for it too.

Yet with the unlikely rise of an openly socialist leader whose authentic, seemingly egoless iconoclasm formed such a refreshing contrast to the personally ambitious, ideologically shape-shifting type, and whose unexpected electoral gains in 2017 seemed to put a genuinely left-wing government within reach, I felt impelled belatedly to join the legions on the doorstep. Not that I was at all convinced that canvassing worked (with reason, it turns out). Like physiotherapy, it is a long-term undertaking, the incremental benefits of which can be difficult to believe in. But everyone seemed to be doing it: not just seasoned activists or political aficionados, and not just one circle of friends, but everyone.

Canvassing isn't a wholly feel-good activity. I was initiated into the art by a more experienced friend one November Sunday afternoon in Battersea. At first, I just followed him around, trying to memorise his openers and copy his doorstep demeanour, hardly speaking but grinning indefatigably. It felt unnatural – illegitimate, even – and often uncomfortable. Most people didn't answer our question about how they would be voting, and many didn't want to talk at all, so having any conversation – even a negative one – was a relief.

One gains confidence quite quickly – perhaps too quickly: soon, I was initiating others. But you begin to feel less self-conscious at the cost of feeling a bit less like yourself. You develop an artificially undaunted and insufferably polite manner to override your misgivings, while the sense of purpose and mild sacrifice can lead you to acquire a regrettably chipper, officious and self-satisfied attitude (after all, you are giving up your Sundays to traipse around for the Greater Good).

In the weeks building up to the election I didn't stray from local London marginals – Putney, Battersea, striking out to Hendon later on – but on polling day itself, informed by Momentum that constituencies in the capital would be over-subscribed and volunteers were needed elsewhere, I took a train to Shoreham-by-Sea, which I knew a little because I have family nearby. My canvassing mentor had some friends in Brighton who had been canvassing in the Tory-held East Worthing and Shoreham constituency for weeks, and the local organisers were optimistic (in the event, the Conservatives increased their already healthy majority by over a thousand votes).

As it was all over the country, the weather was spectacularly grim and unpropitious, but the resulting hardship only heightened our sense of adventure and perception of our own valiance. There was a particular road perpendicular to the seafront – you could look down it and see big, grey-brown waves frenziedly crashing into the shore – where the wind was extreme, aggravating the rain. We had to shelter beside garden hedges to write on our madly flapping sheets before plunging them back into a plastic bag so they wouldn't become illegible.

After an hour or so battling the weather, we would return to a house whose owner had offered it as a makeshift base camp. There, we were fed home-made soup and sandwiches and cake, and made cups of tea and coffee; we could use the bathroom and plug in our phones, sit down, get warm, let our legs dry off a little and generally recharge before heading back out to the front. The intense but also purposeful sociability of the experience gave me that intoxicating sense of strangeness to myself, of distance from my everyday personality – a rare, life-affirming feeling I associate with the otherworldly collectivity of music festivals. But this immediate sense of community was also underpinned by a broader atmosphere of imagined solidarity: one was perpetually buoyed by the thought of the thousands of passionate volunteers who were doing the same thing in similarly dreadful conditions across the country.

We finished up at about 7.30 p.m. – the Shoreham organisers told us that there were no more doors to knock on. Feeling triumphant, we got on a train that was due to arrive at Victoria at 9.58 p.m. As we neared our destination, I received a text from a friend who had been canvassing in Battersea; they were heading to the Labour HQ to watch the exit poll results come in. I looked it up on Google Maps and saw it was right next to

Clapham Junction, where our train was pulling in. We jumped off and raced out of the station to the HQ. Arriving, I recognised it as where I'd been for my first ever canvassing session. Everyone was crowded into a glass-walled conference room, sitting on the floor, eyes glued to the big screen at the front. The room was extremely tense; I was nervous too, but also undeniably – dangerously – elated.

We can skip reminiscences about what happened next – the evening's events are no doubt seared into everyone's memories anyway. Some days later, once the initial winding shock had begun to subside, there was a feeling of bathos and quasi-embarrassment at the apparently deluded futility of the campaigning effort – an effort that had felt all-important, pivotal. Perhaps also the faint feeling of having been misled, or led on.

I go into the detail – the gory arc – of my election experience first because it is a memory that would be easy to misrepresent. The analogy that comes to mind is the self-loathing that can greet you the morning after a party at which you were too chatty. But self-analysis in the throes of a hangover is not known for its lucidity or fairness; I think of that kind of cringing retrospection as the affective opposite of nostalgia, no more trustworthy than its idealising counterpart. If one's sense of the efficacy of doorknocking was inflated at the time, it can be equally distorting to hyperbolise one's earlier benightedness and the pointlessness of the activity in retrospect.

But I also wanted to revisit my experience because I know it is not remotely unique or extreme – quite the opposite. People like me – late arrivals with no prior experience of, and very little exposure to, sustained activism – have been lightly touched by Corbynism, our participation tardy and modest compared to the many who joined or re-joined the Party punctually, in 2015, and to those who devoted hundreds of hours to organising and campaigning. In a sense, we embody some of the paradoxes of the mobilisation Corbyn inspired: fleeting but intense; narrow, demographically and geographically, but numerous; shallow but spirited. In another sense, I take myself and those like me – mild cases – to be encouraging litmus tests. Though inevitably the energy and intensity have faded since last December, I felt, and still feel, affected by what happened: both inspired and traumatised, activated and numbed. I don't yet know – I suppose I'm waiting to find out – how deeply or lastingly, and in what ways, this personal change will manifest in future.

This question about what will endure from that frenetic period and what it portends is, of course, one of the questions we are used to putting to leaders, to those in the Party with power and influence. One scrutinises them in an attempt to sound out their real attitude to the political energy released by Corbyn's tenure – whether they intend to protect and expand it or to oversee its petering out – in order to decide whether, or how much, to trust them, and what one's relation to the Party will be in future. This searching scrutiny of those at the top can be a fraught and painful activity.

Hence it can be a balm – and a productive, rather than avoidant one – to ask the same question of oneself. I take heart from a couple of sentences I came across in *Tribune*'s 'After Corbyn' issue:

> People are changed through their involvement in projects like the ones around Corbyn and Sanders. The process of trying to build a party that can transform a state itself creates a broader capacity in people to look at the world differently.

On the one hand, it is clear that, in strictly political-strategic terms, 2019's electoral mobilisation was a failure. It felt shallow because it was. Secular trends – regionalised economic neglect, the dis-embedding of political parties from civil society, the neoliberalisation of the ideological field – cannot be reversed overnight, or solely with doorstep conversation. But shallow was not all it was.

Canvassing actually reminded me most of all of my time as a Deliveroo rider. The differences are obvious – not least, the difference in reception when you're handing over a miraculously hot takeaway versus brazenly attempting to extract an electoral commitment – but the parallels are perhaps not trivial: going into neighbourhoods one would otherwise have no reason to visit and getting to see where, and to imagine how, other people live, many of them people you would not ordinarily encounter. This remains valuable and edifying.

There is also the common fact of being part of a decentralised group being sent to different locations by a data-driven algorithm. Canvassing prompted the same realisation I'd had Deliverooing in my local area of London a couple of summers ago: I know so little of where I live, let alone of where I don't. Apart from a brief interlude at university, I've lived in the same square mile my entire life, but what is my relationship to my neighbourhood and its community? Such thoughts about late-capitalist urban experience are not new, of course, but they are newly urgent in the wake of a political defeat that has brutally exposed the long-term withering away of social infrastructure that had helped to provide the opportunity and enticement to associate with others – the convening that prepares the ground for organisation around a specific political purpose.

Tribune's reminder that people are changed through involvement evokes something else I hope I have learned from the heady final months of 2019, a lesson I regard as an experiential confirmation of one of the axioms of the socialist worldview: its acknowledgement and celebration of the radical sociality of human consciousness. The experience of having been swept up in a collective project, in a fleeting, superficial but nevertheless impressive mobilisation – not just door-knocking, but meeting, talking, reading, self-educating – has helped to activate dormant politics, which were previously assumed, untried, often inarticulate. Once awakened, these politics were tested, and shaken, by the devastation and disorientation of defeat. In the immediate aftermath, especially as splits and differences emerged between generations and within friendship groups about the nature of the mistakes, the lessons, the solutions, this disorientation tended to express itself among new recruits such as myself in the form of anxious self-probing, an attempt to overcome the rattling sense that I didn't know my politics after all.

The sense of disorientation abides, but recently the question has begun to form itself rather differently: how to relate one's awakened politics to the new conjuncture, the new and continuously evolving reality? This seems to be a question of engagement beyond mere introspection, a question of knowledge and strategy, but most of all one of practice: of how to behave, how to adhere to one's values, so that one can live in the world – help make it a liveable place – and live with oneself.

If one of the fittingly socialist lessons of the 2019 experience is that one's activity with others can initiate inner change and precipitate evolutions of political consciousness and behaviour, the other half of this dialectical truth is that the legacy of Corbynism – the future of what Corbynism was – is not entirely in anyone's hands. One cannot wish a movement into being; one must also wait for it, but not passively. Perhaps one must lie in wait for it, ready oneself. And as with those at the top, the proof will be in the practice of those on the ground – in what I do, you do, we do next.

3
Scotland: Centrism's Bolthole?

Rory Scothorne

Anyone driving through Ayrshire in the south-west of Scotland might encounter a stretch of the A719 known as the Electric Brae.* Here, an almost imperceptible gradient combines with certain features of the surrounding landscape to produce an optical illusion more widely known as a 'gravity hill'. Kill the engine and leave off the brakes, and your car will begin to roll eerily uphill – or rather, will appear to do so as it actually trundles down to a watery terminus in the Firth of Clyde.

A similar confusion occurs when looking at the state of Scottish politics in 2020. Against the backdrop of Westminster's ongoing catastrophe, the continued dominance of a Scottish National Party that proclaims its 'social democratic' values, speaks up for the rights of immigrants and opposes nuclear weapons suggests a near-magical national capacity for progress against powerful countervailing forces. Look closer, however, and gravity's fatal pull begins to show.

---

* With apologies to Andrew Greig: *Electric Brae*, London, 1992.

In 2015, the SNP swept fifty-six of Scotland's fifty-nine Westminster seats on a vaguely anti-austerity platform, drawing in huge numbers of Labour and Liberal Democrat voters as well as many of the new voters who had been politically activated by the 2014 independence campaign. This was seen by many left-wing independence supporters as a modest triumph for the left, rebounding from the British state's 2014 referendum victory and clearing out the Liberal Democrats alongside a sclerotic and right-wing Scottish Labour establishment.

Since then, however, the SNP has diluted rather than consolidated the left-leaning identity that underpinned the independence movement and the 2015 election win, taking Brexit as an opportunity to plant itself more firmly in the liberal, anti-populist and pro-European centre ground. This vision of Scotland as a fortress of bourgeois enlightenment is nothing new. In 1977 Tom Nairn, discussing the party's geopolitical ambitions, wrote that 'the SNP ideologists tend to perceive us as paid-up members of the élite already'; in Nairn's own utopian imagining, Scots were more likely to 'end up as noisy outcasts, breaking the club windows in order to get in',*

Nairn wrote as the radicalism of the Scottish nationalist movement approached its historical peak. In the late 1970s, Labour's fear of SNP gains in its heartlands ensured that a devolved Scottish Assembly appeared to be almost guaranteed. This prospect, combined with a widespread sense of global breakdown and the 'twilight' of British social democracy, provided a horizon-line upon which left-wing nationalists hung extravagant prophecies about Scotland's future. In one article, Nairn described 'a situation where political revolution is a virtual certainty, where the

---

* Tom Nairn, *The Break-up of Britain: Crisis and Neo-nationalism*, London, 1981, p. 193.

forms of the state are likely to alter profoundly in a long period of uncertainty and escalating conflict.'* In another, Neal Ascherson wrote that 'the Assembly is the hole under the fence of the British system, which can only get wider as first the SNP, and then the bolder Scottish socialists, and finally a whole people thrust their way through it.'†

Supporters of Jeremy Corbyn will recognise the way in which the mere hint of an impending transformation blows open the vaults of possibility, releasing long-gestating ideas and infra-structures into the light of day; this constitutive power of a new political horizon, however moderate or speculative in reality, forges new political networks and intellectual sensibilities that tend to outlast disappointment.

When disappointment came in 1979 – in a referendum, major-ity support for the Assembly failed to pass a prohibitive turnout threshold, and Margaret Thatcher took power shortly after – these radical openings slammed shut. But one legacy of this period is a tradition of cross-party work on the Scottish left that is almost entirely absent in England, and a deep left-wing con-sensus in favour of some measure of national self-determination not just as a means of better governance but as a potential vehicle for radicalism.

The Scottish radical tradition which was revived alongside the prospect of devolution in the 1970s is now scattered across the SNP, Scottish Labour, the Scottish Greens and the Scottish Socialist Party, all of which have played prominent roles in the Scottish Parliament. It can be found too in a small set of left-wing counterpublics, from social media networks and online fora such

---

*   Tom Nairn, 'Revolutionaries versus Parliamentarists', *Question* 16, November 1976, p. 4.

†   Neal Ascherson, 'Return Journey', *Question* 1, October 1975, p. 5.

as Bella Caledonia and The Ferret, to campaign groups such as the Living Rent tenants' union, the Common Weal 'think and do tank' and the Radical Independence Campaign.

The new horizons offered by the independence referendum of 2014 gave this tradition a desperately needed shot in the arm. Unionism offered no such generative horizon, and the intellectual and political infrastructure of the anti-independence Scottish Labour left emerged from the referendum as stagnant and cantankerous as before. With most of its natural base already diverted into the independence movement, Corbynism in Scotland produced little in the way of an intellectual or political renewal for Scottish Labour. Richard Leonard's victory over the 'moderate' Anas Sarwar in the 2017 leadership election reflected the moribund status of the party establishment more than any left-wing resurgence.

Much of the SNP's radicalism, meanwhile, is buried in its past, and the only broken windows for which the party can claim credit today are those of Scotland's crumbling local facilities. Far from fighting austerity, the SNP have passed it on to councils: while Holyrood's revenue budget fell by 2.8 per cent between 2013–14 and 2018–19, the Scottish government handed down a 7.5 per cent cut to local authorities over that period. A reduction in the ability of local authorities to adapt to local needs reflects the SNP's 'this far and no further' approach to decentralisation, drawing power towards Holyrood from Westminster and local government alike, on everything from policing to taxation.

It is no bad thing that the Scottish Parliament has continued to decommodify basic services under the SNP, building on an earlier Labour–Liberal Democrat coalition policy of free personal care for the elderly. Free tuition, free prescriptions, free bus travel for young and old and free period products across Scotland (a policy pushed through by Scottish Labour MSP Monica Lennon) all contribute to a renewed vision of social citizenship outside market mechanisms. Each moment of free access, however modest, forms a utopian breach in capitalist realism which allows social demands to be ratcheted up. These rationed glimpses of life beyond market determination supply contemporary Scottish nationalism with much of its remaining left-wing and emancipatory energy.

But declining standards in health and education provide recurring headaches for the party, indicating growing crises within two systems which form the bedrock of devolved administration. There is an element of genuine helplessness here, for the generalised threshing of the UK's social fabric by the post-2007 recession and UK austerity has been only slightly reduced in Scotland by devolution, placing far greater strains on public services than their diminished funding can support. There is only so much that the country's devolved institutions can do against a right-wing UK government which retains key powers over policies such as welfare, immigration, tax and spending. This flattering comparison of domestic inadequacy with neighbouring cruelty allows the SNP to absorb much of the criticism of its record into the broader case for independence.

The vision of independence has also been diluted since 2014. In the aftermath of the Brexit vote, Nicola Sturgeon tasked Andrew Wilson – former RBS economist, SNP MSP and now corporate lobbyist – with chairing the SNP's Sustainable Growth Commission. This was supposed to update the economics of the case for independence, drawing on a range of sympathetic expertise that was noteworthy for the absence of trade union representation. Its report concluded that Scotland could join 'the best small countries in the world' – Denmark, Finland and New Zealand – within a generation, but only through some tough choices.

Two choices in particular stood out: first, deficit reduction through the restriction of public spending increases to 'significantly less than GDP growth' over a five-to-ten-year transition period, which both the Institute of Fiscal Studies and left-wing critics within the independence movement have argued is a recipe for a decade of austerity; and second, the retention of sterling as Scotland's currency without any say in its governance, which some independence supporters have attacked as a further abandonment of economic sovereignty to the UK. In the SNP's positioning, the 'progressive' justification for independence is now rooted more directly in fear of a hard Brexit and popular disdain towards the Conservatives than in any direct challenge to the British economic and political system.

The wider independence movement's self-image of simmering national potential and popular radicalism is also undermined by the realities of the SNP's independence strategy. No matter how great the party's 'mandate' from Scottish voters, the power to hold a binding independence referendum is reserved to Westminster, where the Conservatives' reliance on unionist votes will encourage them to ignore that mandate indefinitely.

Although extralegal alternatives to a legal referendum have been discussed among the wider movement, there is little of the deep and existential cross-class interest in Scottish nationalism that can be found in genuinely revolutionary national movements. Broad aspirations for the 'normality' of nation-statehood – which can also be found among economically anxious 'No' voters – are not matched by the bootstrapping popular will to achieve it.

While this would almost certainly make the eventual winning of independence a historically (and laudably) peaceful affair, it also exposes the relatively shallow justification for it: England's political priorities may be increasingly and painfully divergent from Scotland's, but they do not involve the actual subjugation of the Scottish people to anything approaching colonial rule. If Scotland is a victim, it is a victim of its own relative size and circumspection, of a quiet reluctance to test the depths of its unique identity and collective power: a condition of 'self-colonisation', in Nairn's words, shared with every nation whose middle and working classes have taken, when offered, the opportunities and patronage of a larger, more powerful neighbour, constructing in the process a bridgeway to assimilation which is prohibitively expensive to destroy.

The renewed sense of constitutional disempowerment created by Brexit among Scotland's traditionally cautious middle classes resonates with a deeper and more sustained experience of collective economic marginalisation across both working and middle-class Scots. The Conservatives' removal of support for Scottish industry, combined with their attacks on the public sector during the 1980s, had a genuinely cross-class effect in Scotland. More of the middle class was employed in and around the public sector than in England, and Scotland had fewer private sector options to move into. Devolution's appeal as a middle-class barricade against future disruption in Scotland is obvious in its politicians' and intellectuals' continued enthusiasm for the country's bulging public, third and cultural sectors, all of which provide reliable sanctuaries for the castaways of collapsing academic and journalistic job markets.

But in the world of 'making things' – the essence of Scotland's twentieth-century economic identity – sanctuary is hard to find. Last year, the continuation of Scotland's long-term industrial decline was hammered home through the high-profile but unsuccessful campaign by Unite to save the St Rollox 'Caley' railworks, a fixture of Glasgow's Springburn district since the mid-nineteenth century that was mothballed for want of new investment. The Caley's owners, part of a German-based multinational, chose to concentrate their work in England. They calculated that English yards would be better equipped to service the newly upgraded rolling stock of ScotRail, the Scottish rail company contracted out to Abellio, which is run by the Dutch government.

Meanwhile, on the coast of Fife, the two yards of Burntisland Fabrication or 'BiFab' faced substantial job losses and the threat of mothballing as work dried up. BiFab's transition from fossil fuel infrastructure to renewables connected nicely to the 'Green Industrial Revolution' promised by Alex Salmond during the SNP's successful 2011 Scottish Parliament campaign, but global markets thought otherwise: despite BiFab's proximity to the planned fifty-three-turbine Neart na Gaoithe windfarm off the Fife coast, the vast majority of turbine jackets are to be constructed in Indonesia, with just eight going to BiFab after a sustained campaign by the Scottish Trades Union Congress and GMB.

This is a new and more insidious version of what the Tory politician Walter Elliot once described as the 'denationalisation' of the Scottish economy, fatally undermining cross-party ambitions for renewables-based reindustrialisation. In the 1940s, Elliot was referring to London-based nationalisation which took power away from native Scottish capital; today, the control of Scotland's economy shifts between opaque multinationals.

Scotland's policy ambitions are in many ways those of a typical North European state, yet it lacks the accompanying material supports of a large, high-quality native manufacturing sector, powerful trade unions and a public-spirited, well-resourced bourgeois press that can facilitate nationwide consensus around balanced development. Even Scotland's distinctive elite media is now undergoing the same experience of branch-plant offshoring that it once reported in concerned detail.

This slow collapse in the economic conditions of self-determination offers, however, some paradoxical consolation for the Scottish left. With its fragile industry, political marginalisation and defensive trade unions, Scotland may lack the requisite infrastructure for socialist revival; but in the absence of real state power and confident native capital, it is also lacking in nourishment for an independent and ambitious political right. Instead, the nation's politics are structured around a stifling ideological stalemate, wispily abstracted from political economy, which is often confused with progressive consensus.

This vacuous anti-materialism is what makes the Scottish political system such a secure bolthole of centrism against a global shift towards the extremes. The absence of more vigorous partisan conflict between independent class interests is what allows the SNP – by its very nature, the party most capable of changing its colour to suit a distinctly national political character – such undiminished hegemony.

If there is a more immediate threat to Scotland's bland stability, it comes from independence. The SNP's programme for independence represents a recognition that the first step to independent statehood would be the build-up of a native capitalist class, while demanding 'partnership' – as the Growth Commission report puts it – from the labour movement. Its deficit-cutting plans represent a clear programme of primitive accumulation, redirecting the wealth produced by the Scottish people from public services towards a hoped-for influx of international capital that would quickly make the Scottish Parliament its own.

This presents the Scottish Labour Party with a clear dilemma. Unless it wishes to abandon much of its progressive appeal and compete with the Conservatives for socially conservative unionist votes, its electoral pitch needs to focus on those working-class and left-wing middle-class voters who voted 'Yes' in the independence referendum and now mostly vote SNP or Green. Yet it cannot begin to rebuild its credibility with those voters without a noticeably radical, and highly risky, change of position on the national question.

The Labour Party has thus far tried to fight the SNP by simply outflanking it on the left, with little success. Scotland has two intersecting political cleavages – left/right and Scottish/British – and the left-British demographic is simply too small to sustain a serious challenge to the SNP. Labour has, throughout its history, sought to straddle this territorial divide with a 'Scottish and British' identity, the limitations of which have been exposed in its institutionalisation. The Scottish Parliament's contradictory origins – both in and against the British state – have combined with the rise of the SNP and the rightward, anti-European drift of Anglo-British politics to split Scottish and British identity further apart, leaving Scottish Labour dangling over the chasm, clinging for dear life to the red in the Union Jack.

Labour is highly unlikely to return to power at Westminster without some kind of public compromise with England's proudly reactionary political culture, allowing the SNP to continue knotting leftish liberal democracy and Scottish identity together to maintain its secure position at Holyrood. For those elements of the left who fear a return to the Presbyterian darkness of the 1950s, this is an unappetising recipe for intensified self-colonisation. Scottish politics, surrendered to the SNP but held back from independence, will only stagnate further, and such stagnation is already becoming a breeding ground for the development of our own, indigenous strains of cultural reaction.

Former first minister Alex Salmond is reportedly keen on staging a Holyrood comeback after his acquittal on sexual assault charges, and accuses the party's current leadership of conspiring against him. Some Salmond supporters favour a more radical 'Plan B' approach to independence, involving open confrontation with the British state. Some have also orchestrated a furious backlash against the SNP's attempts to reform the Gender Recognition Act, sharpening a culture war at the heart of Scotland's ostensibly liberal establishment. This is a recipe for vicious internal turmoil equivalent to the struggle of Blair versus Brown. If Sturgeon cannot survive it, the cosmopolitan trajectory of mainstream Scottish nationalism could be redirected into something more populist, exclusionary and socially conservative.

If there is a way out of these dynamics, it may yet go through the British state – but it cannot end there. With the SNP degenerating, there is a clear need in Scotland for the distinctive combination of economic transformation and radical cultural politics that Corbynism articulated. But the Labour left is no use to Scottish socialists if it cannot empathise with and support efforts to break away from the anti-democratic political and media system that spent five years sabotaging Corbyn's chances. And there is much Labour could still do to prove its worth to left-wing independence supporters: through a programme of carefully targeted economic reconstruction and the redistribution of industrial power, a Labour government at Westminster could create in Scotland the conditions for a far more democratic form of political, economic and cultural independence, achieved through the patience and realism that the SNP claims to support.

This could be premised not on outright separation but on loose confederation – though this would require a complex relationship between Scotland, the remainder of the UK and Europe. Scotland could free itself from marginalisation by English majorities without further sacrificing itself to foreign investors, while Scottish Labour could realign itself with its progressive base and create the foundation for a friendly and egalitarian relationship with its neighbours in the former United Kingdom.

This analysis will be tested by the coronavirus crisis. Do the Johnson government's emergency interventions provide fresh resources for a revival of popular left-unionism to rival that which followed the Second World War? While the viral threat may provide a powerful binding agent, the accompanying economic crisis will not. The UK's ruling classes, embracing different forms and identities across nations, have evolved to thrive in those gaps between incorporation and fragmentation, exploiting devolved limits and ambiguities as comfortably as they wield the power of the central executive.

Its working classes have not done the same, and Labour was always naïve to think that it could exploit or manage those contradictions through the trick of 'more devolution'. A world-historic economic crash prompting new conflicts over the distribution of resources and the limits on central power is far more likely to expose than resolve the profound flaws of that system, encouraging rather than slowing Britain's long breakdown. In such circumstances, it is only by seizing the wheel and steering carefully towards a break-up in its own image, rather than gazing aghast at the spectacle of decline, that Labour can reverse its downward slide in Scotland, and Scotland's with it.

4

Why Lexit Was Right

Andrew Murray

Since the financial crash of 2008 there have been two moments – just two – when the European left looked capable of taking the political initiative away from both the mildewed centrists whose neoliberalism led to the crisis and the nationalist authoritarians who have successfully exploited it. One was the advent of a Syriza government in Greece, the other the 'Corbyn moment' in Britain.* Both insurgencies came to grief, for broadly the same reason: an inability or unwillingness by most of the left to think outside the European Union box. Of course, there were numerous contingent factors at play, but the final coup de grâce in either case was administered by the 'European issue', which detached the party leaderships from their working-class supporters.

---

* A left alliance has governed Portugal for several years, with modestly beneficial results but limited international resonance. At the time of writing, Podemos has entered coalition in Spain as a junior partner with the PSOE. How this will fare remains to be seen.

.

Syriza capitulated to the EU's austerity demands in the summer of 2015 despite winning a handsome popular mandate to resist them. Following that debacle, Alexis Tsipras limped on through NATO-and-neoliberal orthodoxy to defeat at the polls. In the UK, Jeremy Corbyn's Labour Party ditched its previous commitment to respect the Brexit referendum result, and instead cleared the way for its reversal through a second public vote, setting its face against the considerable majority of working-class people who had voted Leave. Labour was hammered in the December 2019 general election and the immediate future of 'Corbynism' now hangs in the balance.

One lesson of post-2008 politics seems compelling, then. The socialist left needs to get its head straight about the European Union.

The EU has been anaesthetising European socialism for a long time now. It owes its success as a 'left-wing' project precisely to its pain-killing properties, reconciling the labour movements of Europe to their historic defeat in the 1980s. In Britain, certainly, Euro-enthusiasm was embraced by a movement down on its luck, its self-esteem ebbing. When EU Commission President Jacques Delors charmed the Trades Union Congress in 1988, he did it by retailing the sort of social-democratic palliatives no longer on offer at Westminster. His vision of a 'social Europe' offered not a novel route to socialism, but a cover for discarding an objective which had come to be seen as unattainable in favour of trusting to a saviour from on high who might deliver at least something.

In the years that followed, Labour vacated acres of political space by clinging firmly to the Brussels dispensation, even while the EU was brazenly imposing austerity on Greece, Ireland, Portugal and Italy on behalf of neoliberal orthodoxy. Boris

Johnson charged into that space in the 2019 election campaign, trumpeting the government's greater flexibility to offer state aid to industry and prioritise domestic suppliers in public procurement once clear of EU structures.

Jeremy Corbyn undoubtedly wanted to advocate the same line of policy. But he was doubly stuck. First, Labour had to square a desire to deploy state aid with a commitment to align closely with single-market rules that severely circumscribe it. Second, the Party had painted itself into a corner whereby it couldn't admit that there was *anything* potentially positive about leaving the EU, for fear of alienating impassioned Remainers in London, other big cities and the university towns.

If anyone asks why the Tories outpolled Labour among the working class in 2019, at least part of the answer may be that Johnson was able to pass himself off as wielding nation-state power to protect the economic interests of the people, the traditional tune of social democracy.

Europe used to present more of a problem for the Conservatives than for Labour, from the controversies over the Maastricht Treaty in the early 1990s to David Cameron's cynical decision to call an in/out referendum to appease Farage voters. Two preoccupations of the right powered Tory Euroscepticism: xenophobic nationalism and the hope that, if EU regulations were shaken off, Britain could embrace the free market with even less inhibition than hitherto. However, these attitudes had to be set against the interests of big business and the City in continued EU membership, and reconciled with an electorate that didn't, by and large, share the party's fixation with the issue. Such were the ingredients of a long-running political malaise.

But the Tories have now put their European agonies to rest, at least for the time being. How did they do it? Step one was the termination of the tortured premiership of Theresa May and her replacement by the exuberant Brexiteer-of-convenience Boris Johnson. Step two was Johnson's achievement of a new and improved Brexit deal from the EU and his defenestration of recalcitrant Conservative MPs without regard to service record or heredity, two former chancellors and a Churchill among the vanquished. Step three was a general election sweep of a country drained empty of political hope by Euro-fatigue, on a simple 'get Brexit done' platform.

While Johnson was flushing out the Tories' age-old EU blockages with brio, Labour was succumbing to Euro-paralysis, in large part due to pressure from Party membership and the liberal commentariat. Labour had dodged the Brexit bullet in 2017 only to spend 2019 placing a blindfold over its eyes and yelling 'shoot' at the general election firing squad. The problem wasn't only the convoluted policy that the Party ended up with (a second referendum with a choice between the status quo and a new deal that would look and feel very much like the status quo, with no guarantee that anyone in the proposed Labour administration would actually support the deal negotiated and, in fact, every reason to believe that most ministers wouldn't). It was also the months of agonised indecision that preceded it, and the campaign of parliamentary obstructionism that the Party waged in the meantime.

The story of the period between the relative success of 2017 and the absolute failure of 2019, therefore, is one of Labour's miserable migration from occupying the role of insurgent agent of radical change to appearing to belong to a stonewalling establishment, besotted with parliamentary and legal arcana and incapable of initiative on the issue overshadowing all others in national life.

In a sense, that perception was unfair. A parliamentary opposition doesn't have the weather-making potential of government;

an obligation to obstruct is almost baked into the constitutional conventions of the Commons. Nevertheless, a hung parliament in which a significant minority of the government's own MPs were in open revolt offered opportunities that could have been further exploited, had Labour managed to settle on delivering a withdrawal from the EU on something like the terms offered in the 2017 Manifesto, rather than expending all its energies in trying to block and then reverse the whole process.

Labour's mistake lay in reducing the Brexit crisis to a problem of party management, and of allowing the concerns of the electorate to become somewhat marginal. The Labour membership – weighted towards London and southern England and relatively disconnected from the Party's deindustrialised regional heartlands – was preponderantly pro-Remain, if that was the question being asked. However, members were far keener on securing a Corbyn government than fighting the Brexit referendum all over again. Instead of drawing on that strength and building on the foundation of 2017, the Labour leadership was immobilised by a combination of creeping parliamentary cretinism and the well-funded, well-organised campaign – run mainly by Corbyn-hating New Labour figures – for another 'people's vote'.

The Brexit crisis highlighted another problem besides misapprehension of the EU project, a problem that has been incubating for far longer and is now rampant on the left, namely a confusion between liberalism and democracy, and between liberalism and socialism.

The European Union is liberal in the classical sense of upholding the rights of private property against the state and of entrenching market relationships, and also in the more modern connotation of supporting individual freedoms – including, saliently, the right to live and work anywhere within its borders

– and opposition to gender, ethnic, religious or other forms of discrimination. Its 'internationalism' offers the free movement of people within the Union (if not free movement into it from the rest of the world), as well as mandating the free movement of capital, goods and services.

That makes it good enough for some on the left. But though it may be liberal, the EU is no more than a parody of a democracy, governed by an inaccessible bureaucracy barely answerable to a powerless Parliament. The 'remain and reform' mantra with which left-Remainers concealed their nakedness was absurd. There is no prospect of serious reform in the EU's purpose and functioning, absent the election of Corbyn-type governments in all the decisive countries in Europe: a circumstance which would be as likely to precipitate the end of the EU as presently constituted and its supersession by some form of socialist federation.

Socialism stands for social equality for all. That is a different programme to the individualism embraced by significant strands of the left, sometimes as a substitute for class politics. These demands can doubtless be reconciled, but only through a democratic process. It is the misfortune of the left today that it sometimes appears to prefer the imposition of virtue by decree to the exercise of democracy. How did a movement which had made opposition to 'judge-made law' one of its foundational principles come to support the judicial overruling of elected governments? Any radical Labour government would come to rue the day it conceded so much ground to the apparatuses of unaccountable bourgeois authority.

Tony Blair's response to the 2019 defeat was to urge Labour to unite with the Liberal Democrats, healing the twentieth-century schism between liberalism and social democracy 'to correct the defect from our birth'. Liquidation of independent labour politics through an alliance with a party deeply compromised by its support for austerity, and equipped with a philosophy fundamentally inimical to socialism, would represent not only the culmination of the former New Labour leader's lifework; it would also constitute a serviceable replacement guarantee against left radicalism in government with the EU taken out of the equation.

Nevertheless, there are good reasons to hope that the liberal road will not be the one that Labour takes. Blair used to say that his project would be complete when the Labour Party learned to love Peter Mandelson, an event not now imminently anticipated. Never mind loving Peter, even getting the Labour Party to like Tony seems out of reach.

In January this year, YouGov polled Party members on their attitudes to past Labour leaders. Remarkably, Blair was the only one of thirteen figures stretching back to the 1920s to receive a negative rating: 37 per cent of respondents had a favourable assessment of him and 62 per cent an unfavourable one, a net deficit of 25 percentage points. Even Ramsay MacDonald scraped into positive territory (+ 6), which is more than he deserves. Blair's score contrasts with those for Jeremy Corbyn (+ 42), Ed Miliband (+ 43) and Gordon Brown (+ 32). Harold Wilson scored a sensationally positive rating of 55, although when one reaches that far back in time, the 'don't know/who was he?' replies start to pile up. History primer: Wilson won more general elections than Blair and resisted US blandishments to assist with its invasion of Vietnam.

The same survey also canvassed members' opinions of particular organisations. Unsurprisingly, Labour's two largest trade union affiliates performed best. The 19 per cent of respondents who have a negative view of Unite – the Party's biggest funder and Corbyn's staunchest supporter – are presumably the same

19 per cent who support Labour First and Progress, the two organisations around which the right wing of the Party has coagulated. Labour First represents traditional pro-capitalist Atlanticists, while Progress was the Blairite vanguard in the heyday of New Labour.

If these right-wing factions speak for less than a fifth of the Party, they can console themselves that this is more than the 4.5 per cent which Liz Kendall, their standard-bearer, polled in the 2015 leadership contest. There was no repeat of this derisory outcome in the 2020 leadership election, since for the first time the tradition of Herbert Morrison, Hugh Gaitskell, George Brown, Roy Jenkins, James Callaghan, Denis Healey, Roy Hattersley, Tony Blair and David Miliband was unrepresented on the ballot paper.

Further good news from the YouGov poll is that the non-union organisation which Labour members like best is the Stop the War Coalition (+ 41), followed by Labour Friends of Palestine (+ 35). By contrast, only 17 per cent of Labour members have a positive view of Labour Friends of Israel, the least popular of the campaigns featured, which is perhaps unsurprising given its devotion to banging the drum for a country that has been under hard-right leadership for most of the century and that is engaged, in the West Bank, in an active colonisation programme no less oppressive than other such endeavours throughout history.

The views of Party members should influence the next Labour leader's room for manoeuvre on that aspect of policy which was most important to Jeremy Corbyn, and which provoked the most strenuous opposition to him in the media and within the Parliamentary Party: his anti-imperialism. Solidarity with the Palestinian people, support for the anti-war movement, unwillingness to commit to nuclear destruction, opposition to the

Anglo-American embrace of Saudi Arabia, defence of Venezuela's embattled socialists, scepticism about the further expansion of NATO – these positions are popular with Party members. The new leader will therefore struggle to strike out in a different direction. There will be no support for a Trump war against Iran, nor any other military adventure in the Middle East. Pressure to cut the strings tying British diplomacy to Washington's apron will remain potent within the Party. This shift in sentiment – a direct negation of Blair's foreign policy – may prove to be a significant part of Corbyn's legacy, although not one the right wing will ever be reconciled to.

For the rest, the 'Corbyn project' was a bold attempt to create a new socialism fit for the twenty-first century and an electoral coalition to underpin it, even while under unremitting political fire from the Labour right as well as the avowed enemy. The attempt to reformulate the historic objectives of the labour movement after a prolonged period of retreat, and to defeat the entrenched opposition of a powerful and experienced establishment, lacked nothing in ambition. The dull epigones of a rancid 'extreme centre' are free to crawl over every error, bray at every shortcoming and exult in the superiority of their own Potemkin village programmes. But there is no road back to their comfortable end of history.

Today – the barbarism of Boris Johnson, a carnivalesque synthesis of neoliberalism and authoritarian populism, debauching democracy and inflaming social division. Tomorrow – well, socialism is once again on offer, the lasting achievement of the past four years.

5

Five (Bad) Habits of Nearly Successful Political Projects

Gargi Bhattacharyya

Don't say: legitimate concerns; firm and fair; traditional voters or families or communities; law and order; towns.

Do say: never again; defund; abolish; re-imagine; together.

I should say at the outset that the framing of the question is unsettling. One of the problems about asking about the future of socialism is that it does not sound so promising for fun, for warmth, for lascivious laughter and unbridled hilarity, for sex, for togetherness, for the heady silly seriousness of lives well lived.

Why? Perhaps one problem is that it seems to frame the conversation as a problem to be solved, for and through instrumental means. At worst, it sounds no more than a plan to seize something – the state perhaps, an election maybe – and to postpone all progress until this capture has taken place. Of course, this

murmur of desperate instrumentalism is most pronounced where
I live – in Britain – where 'socialism' is all too often code for
'winning a first-past-the-post election to sneak in some redistribution without scaring the middle ground'.

There is a gap between the energetic and varied attempts to
build Jerusalem here on earth and the often much more bad-
tempered attempts to think about the future of the Labour Party.
As so many others have said, the Corbyn moment brought these
two largely separate projects together, briefly. And fractiously.
And perhaps always impossibly.

However, this was the first time in my life when electoral politics was not presented as a necessary lowering of our expectations.

Whatever else we say to each other, perhaps we could hold on
to this point? Perhaps reframing grown-up politics as asking for
less, perhaps even training ourselves to want less, may quieten
the monstering by popular media, but it is unlikely to serve as a
model for transforming society. It probably is not even a model
for winning elections. Socialism must be more and better than
this. In this spirit of trying not to fight each other to the death, I
offer here a few thoughts on what the British left, if such a thing
exists, has been doing wrong, framed in a manner designed to be
enraging to all sides.

Bad habit no. 1: too much talk about 'the media'

It is hard for those who witnessed the behaviour of the British
media during the 2019 election and in the years of the Corbyn
leadership to downplay the role of the media in political life.
Clearly, and unlike in the 2017 election, the continuous onslaught
of character assassination and outright lies shaped the extent of
the Labour defeat. Yet the fascination with the mainstream media

also works against the development of our political imaginations. For some, it reveals a deep wish to go back to 1997. For others, it chimes with a political training that focuses almost exclusively on 'controlling the narrative'. Socialism must be about more than this, surely. Perhaps we might park our concerns about the media until we have worked out what might be required for us all to stay alive in this next period. The future of socialism might depend more on the second bad habit than the first.

Bad habit no. 2: too much focus on capturing the state and assuming all will then be well

Electoral politics demands some attempt to win elections. Even I understand this. But the creation of electoral machines in the late twentieth and early twenty-first centuries has helped to discredit mainstream politics. Perhaps popular culture refracts this better in the US, with the disaffection with both Bill Clinton and Barack Obama seen in popular films and TV series such as *Primary Colors*, *The Ides of March* and *The Politician*. But Britain is far from immune to the 'none of the above, they are all crooks' approach to political engagement.

In response, we have tended to return to the view that 'we' have better ideas and the only hurdle is persuading the electorate to let us try them out. I wonder if this merits more scrutiny. Often, we don't seem to have much more imagination than our opponents, and certainly are no more adept at communicating our world-changing ideas to others. Of course, we like to claim a monopoly on fairness and justice, but these are old refrains without much excitement in the telling. We often don't seem very interested in how big conceptual objectives might be operationalised, or in the challenges associated with trying to operationalise policy ideas in our highly dispersed, overly surveilled times. Perhaps it would help to think more about how hard it is to do these things and to acknowledge more openly the additional and more recent challenges to doing anything through the established practices of politics. I doubt that anyone will believe what we say unless we do this.

Bad habit no. 3: too little attention to how people are living – barely

I did not expect to live to see the results of the grinding hardship that has become unremarkable in Britain today. But here it is: widespread food insecurity, including for children; a housing crisis that forces more people onto the streets and their friends' sofas, and which consigns many more to inadequate, health-destroying and sometimes downright scary places to live; a benefits system designed to punish, which has led to the deaths of some of the most vulnerable; an all-round lowering of expectations so that the entire economy comes to resemble the mixture of hustle, violence and just-getting-by of war societies, with the most unscrupulous making a killing and everyone else borrowing to keep afloat.

We have learned that many do not believe any policy intervention can make things better for them. Distrust of the political class and, perhaps more importantly, painful experiences of interacting with the agents of the state from birth onwards can suffocate hopes of transformation through political institutions. As this deadening of hope has been employed as an active technique of austerity, the presentation of an alternative state-led machinery of poverty reduction appears implausible. After decades of being trained to expect less and less from formal institutions of government – a training achieved through a combination of political rhetoric and active impoverishment – the belief in the ability of political programmes to deliver something better has been broken. At the very least, perhaps we should devote some attention to the manner in which active impoverishment has been deployed as a tool to dismantle popular belief in democracy.

Bad habit no. 4: too great a belief that socialism has been done before in Britain

This idea cuts to the heart of generational divides in political imagination. Much – perhaps too much – talk about socialism in this country rests on a not-so-hidden assumption that something like socialism has been done here before. Mainly, I think this is regarded as no more than the NHS and the welfare state. Sometimes it might also include a wider nostalgia for social democracy. What it misses is the variableness of supposedly universal access, the violence and disenfranchisement built into the distribution of social goods even when access to such goods has been relatively buoyant, and the punitive character of the state in more recent interactions.

Perhaps we need more disruption and less continuity. When we think of people as nostalgic, perhaps they are just fed up.

Bad habit no. 5: too little attention to how things might get done

This problem is not only an electoral concern – although clearly it is that as well. Not only is state support inadequate for many, even in times when the welfare state has been broader and deeper, but it is also an unconvincing vehicle for the tasks we must achieve together in this most unpredictable and alarming of presents. I realise I am dangerously close to sounding like the disrupter boys of the right, but perhaps there is something in their instincts. The British left, which remains tied to electoral aims, has translated this concern into a question of marketing. We want to do good – so we must persuade the voters that we can be trusted sufficiently with the budgets and the bureaucracy to deliver that good.

But perhaps we do not know how to make things happen – and the uncertainty and nerviness caused by this half-articulated realisation haunts political possibility in our time.

Could we make new habits?

Instead of dwelling on 'electoral' or 'self-organised', perhaps it is more useful to think about the world we are entering and how we might imagine mutuality, survival and justice there. We are entering a world more frightening and dangerous than any I have experienced. A global economic crash beyond anything in modern history. A continuing pandemic met with increasingly militarised and repressive methods of behaviour management, all refracted through resurrected and revamped biologism and racist essentialism.

The socialism we imagine for this era must address a widespread longing for safety without resorting to carcerality or militarisation, or the policing of everything. It is a socialism that must grapple with the likelihood that those under forty imagine the state as police violence – maybe also as healthcare and taxation and public provision, but always the uneven dispensation of violence.

It demands a re-imagining of economic life – which may well

require us to institute a refreshed, if not totally new, language. So perhaps – instead of our habitual talk about equality and distribution that has been so successfully turned against us, with the violence of racialised and other divisions used to delimit who can access 'equality' and where the pool of those receiving any (re)distribution might lie – we might think again.

Previously our language of 'values' also implied, or spoke overtly of, modes of operation. Equality not only signalled an aspiration and attitude to the value of all human life, it also informed a set of practices about how to organise the world and how to model institutions that registered the inherent equality of all people.

Although equality retains its emotional and ethical appeal, I don't think we can rely on this framing to communicate an effective broader practice. The misuse of the word, including through shallow bureaucratic practices and the cruelties of austerity, combined with the growth of an everyday consciousness (among the young at least) that 'equality' for some has masked dehumanisation for others, means that our championing of this principle no longer differentiates us from others. More than this, the claim of pursuing equality has lost much of its operationalising credibility. People are painfully aware that formal equality is implemented in ways that feel like punishment for many – while the underside of formal equality via bureaucracy has resulted in exclusion, destitution and abandonment for those deemed beyond the reach of such measures.

The rush of solidarity in movements against state racism and police violence, as well as the earlier shift towards practical migrant solidarity, the resurgence of feminisms that resist carcerality and the significant turn away from dull compulsory heterosexuality among the young all indicate a lived critique of equality as an enforced (if fantastical) homogenisation. At the very least, we need to adjust our language of political dreaming to fit the world that those longing for freedom seek to build. This goes beyond articulating aspiration – although that would not hurt – and requires us to enter the zone of practice, of how we make ideas into ways of doing.

I realise there is a gap between this way of thinking and the demands of electoral politics. Key elements of our collective survival, such as the attempt to reconcile the need for employment with the threat of environmental destruction under the terms of a Green New Deal, seem impossible without the most top-down of policy formulations. Other urgent questions – around social care, health provision, education – seem impossible to address unless we promise to buoy up the crumbling systems of almost-provision. The electoral left is saddled with the failures of state practice even when they are not our failures – perhaps then most of all, because our alternative is so easily regarded as more of the same.

However, and despite our habits and the relentless time pressure of electoral preparation (because another exam is always just around the corner), perhaps we might think again about the language we use to bridge values, aspirations and operationalisation: those key words that bring people around, both to seeing what we want and to glimpsing how that world might be made.

My suggested starting point is to revisit our values through the lenses of mutuality, survival and repair, not only as affective languages – although, of course, these offer important indications of how the future might feel – but also as a reframing of economic and social life. Mutuality – meaning how we are in thrall to and interdependent with each other – always and in all things. Survival as both a recognition of the catastrophic threat to life on the planet and the fact that this catastrophe has been business as usual for much of the world long before this. Repair as a reckoning with what is owed and to whom – and what can never be repaid but which must be repaired if we are ever to achieve mutuality and survival.

Each of the three terms suggests both ethics and action: techniques for collective well-being and methods of re-making collective practice. I suggest these only because there are already experiments in building and sustaining decent lives in harsh times that make use of these terms, as both values and operational practices, ways of thinking but also ways of doing. What might it mean to build a socialist project around these familiar yet different value/practice terms?

6
Losing the Air War
Tom Mills

The media establishment poses a serious obstacle for moderate social-democratic, let alone socialist, politics. This is a longstanding problem, brought sharply into focus by recent events, and one to which the left has yet to develop a satisfactory response, in terms of either policy or strategy. The rapid change to our communicative systems, and the extraordinary power of the digital platforms, however, demand an urgent response.

Though often overlooked by political economists, the shifts in the ownership and organisation of media institutions in the latter decades of the twentieth century were an important aspect of the neoliberal turn that fundamentally weakened the left. The decades immediately following the Second World War had been characterised not only by a strong labour movement, which shaped the structures and culture of state and quasi-state institutions, but also by a more politically balanced media system.

As one would expect in a capitalist press, Tory-supporting newspapers were always ahead of Labour-supporting papers;

from 1945 to 1970 just over half of the newspaper market by circulation backed the Conservative Party, while the remainder favoured either Labour, the Liberals, or remained neutral. However, from the 1970s onwards, a series of closures, takeovers and mergers, and associated editorial changes, saw a marked shift to the right in the industry which helped propel Margaret Thatcher to power.

In 1969, Rupert Murdoch had taken control of the *Sun* – formerly the *Daily Herald*, which was once a hugely popular paper and an organ of the labour movement – and transformed it into a populist right-wing outlet. Thatcher's coterie developed a close alliance with Murdoch and his editors, as well as with the traditional organs of popular conservatism: the *Mail* and the *Express*. Together these titles formed a potent machinery of reactionary propaganda. The proportion of the newspaper market supporting the Conservative Party shot up from around half to between 70 per cent and 80 per cent. The alliances forged, and the backroom deals made, between media owners and politicians in those years have since been revealed by the Leveson Inquiry and official documents disclosed under the thirty-year rule. As was suspected but always denied, Thatcher supported Murdoch's bid for *The Times* and *The Sunday Times* in 1981, and his right-wing stranglehold on the industry was later secured with a victory over the print unions in the Wapping dispute of 1986.

Recent research examining the *Sun*'s endorsement of the Conservatives in 2010 and of Labour in 1997 estimated that each delivered over half a million votes, without any underlying change in readers' political attitudes.* The latter endorsement

---

* Aaron Reeves, Martin McKeeb and David Stuckler, ' "It's the *Sun* Wot Won It": Evidence of Media Influence on Political Attitudes and Voting from a UK Quasi-Natural Experiment', *Social Science Research* 56, March 2016.

had been secured by Tony Blair's assiduous courting of Rupert Murdoch and for a period New Labour reversed the usual political balance of the British press, at least in terms of partisan electoral support. In 2001, the Blairites were even able to secure the support of the *Express*. Labour's rightward shift, accelerated and consolidated by Blair, was in part a strategic response to media power (insofar as capitulation can be considered strategic): the fear of being monstered by Britain's unscrupulous reactionary press served as an opportunity and alibi for Blairite policy and the centralisation of power within the Party.

While the press shifted sharply to the right from the 1970s, broadcasting lagged behind as a legacy of the social-democratic era, but it would follow. The UK's broadcasting system had become progressively more commercialised since the 1950s when advertising-funded commercial television first emerged as a rival to the state broadcaster, and commercial radio followed in the 1970s. But the broadcasting system that operated up to the 1980s was a mixed economy underpinned by a strong public service ethos and regulatory structure, and it contained pockets of genuine political independence and creativity. That was all swept away by late Thatcherism, with both the passing of the Broadcasting Act 1990 – leading to the death of the innovative and independent regional ITV companies – and the introduction of external commissioning at the BBC, along with an internal market and the centralisation of editorial and managerial control.

Socialists have too often neglected media and communications as a second-order issue compared with material concerns, or placed too much faith in the natural capacity of people to resist smears and misinformation. Of course, we all question what we read or watch, drawing on our own knowledge, experiences and networks. But our capacity to do so is always limited by the power of states, corporations and political elites to dominate the communicative environment, and to set the political agenda and the terms of debate. The media, rather like the state, represents a terrain weighted against us, which we cannot afford to ignore if we are serious in our ambitions.

The rise of digital platforms, and the crisis in conventional news media business models, are in the process of profoundly reshaping our system of media and communications – but not necessarily for the better. In March 2016, Jeremy Corbyn remarked in an interview with *Jacobin* magazine that the declining influence of the *Sun* and the BBC, and the opportunities presented by social media, meant that it was much easier to reach people with left ideas than it had been in 1983. The extraordinary 2017 general election result, which reversed years of electoral decline for the Labour Party, seemed to vindicate this; being all the more remarkable for having seemingly circumvented an overwhelmingly hostile media apparatus. But if 2017 seemed to break a spell, 2019 was a rude awakening. The negative treatment of the Labour Party by the media was even more extreme in the 2019 election than in 2017.*

As ever, the power of the media is difficult to disentangle from other factors, but it is very clear that politically motivated smears and misinformation played an important role in the defeat of Corbynism. Take the Labour antisemitism scandal, which despite having no sound evidential basis dominated headlines for years, and featured prominently in the 2019 election campaign. Even

---

* David Deacon, Jackie Goode, David Smith, Dominic Wring, John Downey and Christian Vaccari, 'General Election 2019 Report 5', Loughborough University Centre for Research in Communication and Culture, 7 November – 11 December 2019.

respected broadsheet and broadcast media departed from basic professional standards in their reporting, and as a result of relentless exposure to the issue, British Jews came overwhelmingly to believe that the Party in general was institutionally antisemitic, and even that Corbyn himself was an antisemite. Meanwhile, the broader public thought that on average a third of Labour members had been suspended over the issue.*

With Corbynism roundly defeated, where does this leave the left on the question of the media? The legacy is fairly modest. There were some notable achievements in building up left outlets: Novara, the *Canary*, *Tribune* and *New Socialist*, for example. But not nearly enough was done by the Labour Party under Corbyn to foster socialist media; the focus instead was on classic strategic communications and disseminating left content through digital platforms.

Neither was much headway made on policy. The 2017 Manifesto laid out the same position, basically, as the 2015 Manifesto, and was in fact much more muted in its political rhetoric. The commitments in relation to the press that came out of the Leveson Inquiry were maintained, but unlike in 2015 there was no reference to the 'unaccountable power' and 'undue influence' of media owners, and there was much more concern about the future of the industry. The 2019 Manifesto was similar, but included a reference to addressing the tech giants' advertising monopoly and establishing an inquiry on 'fake news'.

---

*   Jamie Stern-Weiner and Alan Maddison, 'The Myth of a "Labour Antisemitism Crisis"', in Jamie Stern-Weiner, ed., *Antisemitism and the Labour Party*, London, 2019; Justin Schlosberg and Laura Laker, 'Labour, Antisemitism and the News: A Disinformation Paradigm', Media Reform Coalition, mediareform.org.uk, September 2018; Greg Philo, Mike Berry, Justin Schlosberg, Antony Lerman and David Miller, *Bad News for Labour: Antisemitism, the Party and Public Belief*, London, 2019.

The most significant development came in August 2018 with Corbyn's Alternative MacTaggart lecture, in which he argued for the democratisation of the BBC and the establishment of a British Digital Corporation. A number of the candidates to replace him as leader also addressed the question of media reform, which became much more prominent an issue in the aftermath of the general election. Both Clive Lewis and Rebecca Long-Bailey pledged to reform the BBC radically, devolving and democratising programme making. Long-Bailey promised what *The Sunday Times* referred to as 'the biggest change to the BBC's relationship with the state since it was founded in 1922'. Even Lisa Nandy broke with centrist tradition by floating plans for reform.

Notably, however, Sir Keir Starmer made no statement on the issue. This does not bode well, especially given that, insofar as Starmer's supporters have offered anything approaching a political strategy, it seems to rest on offering a 'credible' candidate in the hope of attracting more favourable media coverage. It is worth noting how close this is to the 'soft left' strategy of the Party under Neil Kinnock and Ed Miliband. In any case the basic challenges remain, and in my view the task of the left in the coming years is twofold: first, to build up its own media infrastructure; and second, to set out a positive policy agenda for twenty-first-century public media.

On the first, it is pure fantasy that the existing media structures will ever treat the left fairly, and it is simply not possible for an effective and mature left-wing movement to exist in any sustainable fashion without its own media and communications. At present there are far too few outlets, and those that do exist have far too few resources. We cannot afford to rely on voluntarism. All socialists should provide financial support to left media. In addition, it will be necessary for socialists to start to think seriously about developing their own platforms, as well as making use of commercial platforms as best they can. Competition with either the mainstream news media or the platform giants is not a realistic prospect, but it is imperative that alternatives are developed while state power remains out of reach.

The second priority is developing and effectively disseminating an agenda for media reform that can respond to the profound failings of our media system – including public broadcasting – as well as the serious threat that platform capitalism poses to human freedom. A radically reformed BBC should be a central component of a new public digital ecosystem in the UK.

Though developments were interrupted by the COVID-19 pandemic, in the course of the 2019 general election the Johnson government sought repeatedly to intimidate public media, and afterwards moved quickly against the BBC, in particular with a consultation on the decriminalisation of licence fee non-payment and a war of words waged principally via the stenographers at *The Times*. The response of liberals and sections of the left was to panic and to leap to the defence of the BBC with sentimental pronouncements about public service and portentous references to Fox News.

Whatever Dominic Cummings's intentions, the government is not in a position to abolish the licence fee system. It is protected under the BBC's Royal Charter that runs to 2027, and it cannot be touched in its mid-term review. The Conservative government's immediate intention, therefore, is to reduce the BBC's income further, and to appoint a politically compliant BBC chair to serve alongside the new director general Tim Davie, who before joining the BBC was a PepsiCo marketing executive and active Conservative Party member. The BBC's independence may be under threat but its existence is not, at least for now. The task

of the left in the years ahead, therefore, is to win the arguments
around the BBC before 2027. This means addressing the longstanding problems with its governance, but more importantly
setting out a positive agenda for digital public media.

Ultimately, the goal should be the establishment of an ecosystem of non-commercial producers that are independent from
both the state and commercial oligarchies, and which can harness
the expertise and creativity of workers to produce technology,
information and culture which will be freely available to the public. This will require a devolved, democratic, public framework
for journalism and cultural production, fostered by the existing
public service broadcasters and administered by a new public
media funding body and regulator. Meanwhile, a new British
Digital Corporation (or Cooperative, as Dan Hind prefers)
would produce public digital technology and infrastructure for
the public good.* The market-first media system – a legacy of
neoliberalism – is undermining universal access and hindering
creativity and innovation. It will need to be overhauled.

The global media and communications system is currently
undergoing a profound process of change and it is imperative
that the left effectively intervenes. Capital seeks to monetise education, culture and creativity, either by building paywalls around
'content' or via complex systems of user surveillance for targeted advertising and commercial data analytics. The left's vision
should be to open up information and culture to everyone in a
form that allows us, individually and collectively, to control the
structure of our digital commons.

---

* Dan Hind, 'The British Digital Cooperative: A New Model Public Sector
Institution', common-wealth.co.uk, 20 September 2019.

7

The Defeat of Youth

Keir Milburn

Discussion of the 2019 general election has been dominated by a geographical story: the loss of the so-called 'Red Wall' of traditional Labour seats in the Midlands and northern England. In fact, as many have pointed out, 2019 represented something of a return to the long-term trend of defection from Labour in such areas. In this context, it is Labour's remarkable performance in the 2017 general election that requires explanation, despite vigorous attempts from the right and centre to eliminate this subject from discussion. The increase in Labour's vote share in 2017, the largest since 1945, not only confounded the post-1997 decline in Labour's fortunes but also bucked the post-2008 trend of near collapse among comparable parties in Western Europe. The responsibility for this surge lies predominantly with the young.*

---

*   The idea of increased youth turnout in 2017, the so-called Youthquake, has caused some controversy. While the British Election Study cast doubt on the phenomenon, a later study from the University of Essex provided evidence it had actually taken place. Either way, nobody disputes that increased vote share among the young drove Labour's good performance.

Neither the 2017 nor the 2019 election can be understood without reference to the political generation gap, which is common to the last two elections but does not predate them.

While in 2010 Labour had just a 1 per cent lead over the Conservatives among eighteen to twenty-four-year-olds, by 2017 this had risen to 35 per cent. In that election, for every additional ten years of age, a voter was 9 per cent less likely to vote Labour. Among over sixty-fives the Conservatives led by 36 per cent. The age divide in the 2019 election followed a broadly similar pattern, with a Labour lead of 43 per cent among the youngest cohort and a Tory lead of 47 per cent among the oldest. Although Labour lost some votes among all cohorts, the biggest change from 2017 was among thirty-five to fifty-four-year-olds, where Labour's vote fell by 11 points and the Conservatives' rose by 3.[*]

The scale of the political generation gap that emerged in 2017 and largely persisted through the 2019 election is historically unprecedented. Indeed, it is so significant that it can explain, to a large degree, the geographical divide in voting. The last twenty years have seen a steady increase in the old-age dependency ratio – which measures the proportion of over sixty-fives in comparison to the working-age population – in the villages and small towns where Labour struggled. As the young leave to pursue job opportunities in the larger towns and cities, a self-reinforcing dynamic of age segregation emerges and smaller towns become less and less attractive to the young. The conclusion is obvious:

---

[*] Jeremy Gilbert has suggested that the older end of this cohort was particularly susceptible to media attacks on Jeremy Corbyn and, in particular, the use of the proposal for a second Brexit referendum as a wedge issue to split Labour's 2017 electoral coalition: Gilbert, 'It Was the Centrist Dads Who Lost It', opendemocracy.net, 13 January 2020. Voter demographics from Ipsos MORI and YouGov.

the key to understanding the 2019 election lies, beyond all other things, in the political gulf between the generations.

The political generation gap is all the more intriguing given its sudden emergence across many different countries at roughly the same time. In the first months of 2020 alone, the youth vote drove Sinn Féin's shock win in the Irish general election while the age divide dominated the US Democratic Party presidential primaries. This phenomenon can only plausibly be explained with reference to an event that caused rapid change on an international scale: the financial crisis of 2007–8.

Since 2008, the political views of the young and old have diverged because their material interests have diverged. This situation has been long in the making but the financial crisis and its aftermath accelerated and crystallised the process of generational political divergence. The core of current right-wing electoral coalitions comprises propertied pensioners and home-owners at or near the end of their working lives.* The material interests of this cohort are tied to the value of residential real estate and, because their pensions are invested in stock markets, the performance of the financial sector. The material interests of the propertyless young are opposed to those of this older cohort. Their incomes are reliant on wages and social spending, while their well-being is determined by the cost of living, of which housing costs are the most significant element.

These divergent material interests have led each generation to develop very different impressions of the state of the world, how the economy is doing, and so what the future might hold. The huge disconnect between the indices of the financial sector and indicators linked to the 'real economy' prior to the 2020

---

* Around 75 per cent of UK pensioners own their own homes. Pensioners who rent are no more likely to vote Conservative than younger voters.

pandemic suggests economic growth in the UK was based on a fantasy. Stock prices were at levels that would normally indicate a booming underlying economy, but measures such as GDP, business investment and wage growth indicated a climate of stagnation. Policy response to the 2008 crisis, such as quantitative easing, pushed oceans of free money into the financial sector, which flowed from there into stocks, bonds and property. On the other hand, the 2010s also saw the weakest wage growth since the Napoleonic Wars. When the eyes of young and old are fixed on very different sectors of the economy, it is little wonder there is so much mutual incomprehension between the generations. But while we can understand how divergent perceptions arise, we should not treat them as equally valid.

Within months of the 2019 election, the coronavirus crisis revealed the illusory nature of many aspects of the economic picture embraced by the affluent elderly. The stock market collapse removed the 'gains' of the past decade, while the poor conditions suffered by young precarious workers became hard to ignore once they were identified as a key vector for the spread of the virus. Far from being in rude health, the pre-pandemic economy was brittle, over-indebted and already on the brink of collapse.

In the longer term, the current Boomer worldview will be even more sorely tested by the inevitable intensification of the climate crisis. While some on the ethno-nationalist right, such as Donald Trump and Jair Bolsonaro, are overt climate change deniers, the views of the wider right rest upon implicitly denialist foundations. In fact, Boomer affluence is intimately tied up with the denial of climate science. Current valuations of fossil fuel companies, and so the levels of contemporary stock markets and pensions, assume that all accessible hydrocarbon fuel reserves will be burned. Doing so would end human civilisation. The scale and pace of emissions reductions now required to limit the climate catastrophe are so significant that it is hard to imagine any version of the future in which Labour's defeat in the 2019 election is not seen as a can-kicking disaster.

On the other hand, the crises and problems that pushed the young leftwards are not going away. It seems likely that, while the foundations of the world views of most young people will be confirmed by the events of the next ten years, the same will not hold for the views that currently predominate among the elderly. Many of those positions will become increasingly unsustainable as the decade moves on. In the long run, you can't gaslight physics. The challenge for the left is to predict the events that might confound current right-wing dogma and to develop strategies for interrupting the ideological reproduction of the right. Grasping how material interests are articulated politically will be a key component of breaking a section of older voters away from Conservatism.

One's conception of one's material interest is inherently linked to one's sense of social and political possibility. Individuals have multiple competing interests; they act on those that seem linked to a viable and attractive future. Since 2008 there has been a generational divergence not just of immediate material interests but also around what seems socially and politically possible. A reversion to the pre-2008 status quo and the aspirational life course attached to it may still seem viable to those whose interests have been protected by bank bailouts and quantitative easing, but for the young that line of history is over. Millennials (those aged roughly twenty to forty) are predicted to be the first generation for hundreds of years to have lower lifetime earnings than the previous two generations. The collapse of belief in what we might call neoliberal aspiration among the young – namely the idea that playing by the rules will lead to ever greater levels of consumption – has created scope for left-wing visions of the future to flourish.

Labour's 2019 Manifesto contained an offer to older voters to reframe their material interests in line with those of their younger relatives. The policy of free care for the over sixty-fives and a £100,000 cap on personal contributions to other lifetime care costs, for instance, undermines the idea that equity withdrawal from expensive homes is the only way to guarantee the care the elderly need in old age. Policies to break with the regime of asset-based welfare – in which the middle classes are encouraged to acquire assets to insure themselves against risk, allowing neoliberal governments to cut social security – should remain a central plank of Labour's policy agenda. But while Labour tried to reshape material interests it did not succeed in reshaping what seemed politically possible among the cohorts it needed to win over.

One of the greatest strengths of Corbynism was its ability to draw innovative policy from the new ecosystem of academics and think tanks that Jeremy Corbyn's leadership helped create. Politics can extend the boundaries of what seems possible, and the Corbynite approach certainly appeared to do so, among the young at least. The day-to-day functioning of parliamentary politics, however, involves constant compromise with the status quo, constraining the left's sense of possibility. It is difficult for politics exercised solely in this sphere to escape the conservative framing of a tendentious media, skewed rightwards by oligarchic ownership. Moreover, the only parliamentary option available to a non-governing party is to prevent change rather than create it. Corbyn's near victory in 2017 shortened the apparent time-frame for his immediate political project. This shift trapped Labour into an almost exclusively parliamentary focus, thwarting ambitions to turn the Party into something akin to a social movement and leaving the leadership vulnerable to leverage by the right of the Parliamentary Labour Party.

If parliamentary politics tends to face inwards, towards the existing sense of the possible, then social movements and extra-parliamentary politics have traditionally provided avenues for the left to face the other way, and develop strategies for 'inventing the future'. Over the last three hundred years, the big leaps forward in our collective sense of the politically possible have come from radical social movements, alongside working-class organisation. It seems unlikely that many wealthier pensioners will be won away from the right until events place the future they envision even further into doubt.

As attention moves away from parliamentary politics, where little can be achieved for several years, the space will open up for a renewed movementist turn on the left through a strategy of what is being called 'deep organising'.* This strategy will involve serious efforts both to extend union organising in the workplace and to build new organisations in wider society, such as the rapidly expanding social union ACORN. The first task of such a strategy will be to solidify the grip of socialist ideas on the young following Generation Left's first big defeat.† The second task will be to extend these projects to the more deprived parts of the 'Red Wall' regions. Overcoming the problem of geographical age segregation will not be easy and it may initially involve projects on a fairly small scale, but it is hard to see any other route to bridging the generation gap that is currently dominating politics.

---

* On the difference between shallow mobilisation and deep organising, see Jane McAlevey, *No Shortcuts: Organizing for Power in the New Gilded Age*, Oxford, 2016.

† Generation Left names not just the current left tendency of the young but also the political project to develop and assert a new left politics adequate to its experiences.

8
A Study in the Politics and Aesthetics of English Misery
Owen Hatherley

The first record I played after the December 2019 election was *The Smiths*. I'm not entirely sure why – something about the particular misery of that event, and the sense that we would now have to suffer through a long, deep slog without an obvious end-point, and the feeling that England and Englishness had won some sort of decisive victory. It always seemed improbable, the notion that Britain – by now, with the non-participation of Scotland – was about to embark on an experiment in multicultural radical social democracy, and if you want to luxuriate in the awfulness of England, that's what the entire sound and aesthetic of the Smiths was all about. Nostalgia, guilt, repression, a scab-pulling adolescence now dragged well into pension age.

The other reason was to try and understand something of what had just happened, because the political trajectory of Steven Morrissey seemed to mirror that of large swaths of the North of England – from a kind of anti-Thatcherite left to a proudly racist,

little-Englander right. Here perhaps was the location of a key to
the events, more useful than George Orwell or any 'condition of
England' novel – an awful meeting of the pop culture of affluence, the refusal of maturity, legislated nostalgia, endemic racism
and aestheticised bleakness.

It is conventional to use nostalgia for the Second World War
as an explanation for the particular kind of nationalism that has
gripped England and Wales in the last decade or more. And the
tropes of that war, some of them wholly invented, have indeed
been dominant in post-New Labour Britain-without-Scotland,
from Boris Johnson's conscious modelling of his persona on
Winston Churchill – who now has an entire section of books
to himself in the popular high street bookstore, Waterstone's – to
the recent revival of the Keep Calm and Carry On poster, never
actually distributed in wartime.

The generation that fought the Second World War – and subsequently built some kind of welfare state – is mostly dead. The
overwhelming generational politics of the referendum and the
2017 and 2019 elections, with their supermajorities for the left
among the under forties and hegemony for the right among the
over sixties, demonstrates a profound political shift among people born between 1945 and 1965; as Susan Watkins points out,
even Johnson is Churchill with a 'Beatles mop'.*

The importation of the American term 'Boomers' removes the
reference to the 'baby boom' from the original terminology and
shortens it to imply those that were *born into the boom* – an era
of full employment, abundant cheap housing and free education,
in the war's aftermath. But if you spend your time scouring the

* Susan Watkins, 'Beyond Brexit', *New Left Review* 121, January–February
2020. One could also point out that the *Express* and *Mail*'s 'Big Ben Must Bong
for Brexit' campaign sounds like one of Marc Bolan's gleeful nonsense lyrics.

many Facebook groups where people of this cohort share their disdain for the young, there is no sense that they feel themselves to be the beneficiaries of historical good fortune, or to be in any way privileged. We had it shit, so should they. And who better to explain this scenario than Morrissey?

Morrissey is an extreme example of a common type from the period. Born into a working-class Manchester household of Irish immigrants in 1959, he was brought up in council housing in Hulme and Stretford, and failed his eleven-plus exam – but he then rather spectacularly rose out of the proletariat through the mass media, first as a jobbing music journalist, writing a book about the New York Dolls and another about James Dean, and then as a peculiar kind of pop idol, arguably the founding figure of English indie music. The Smiths, the band he formed in 1982 with Johnny Marr, mounted a deliberate stand against the contemporaneous modernism of British pop culture, particularly in Manchester, where their melodic, nostalgic approach was designed to stand out both from the Bauhaus-derived aesthetic and electronic sound of Factory records and from the abrasive neo-Vorticism of the Fall.*

After a lengthy and largely undistinguished solo career, Morrissey has recently been best known for becoming explicit about his far-right political sympathies, something which had long been suspected but came out in the open when he started wearing, at public appearances in 2018, a badge of the fascist group For Britain. This sect was founded a year earlier by a politician, Anne Marie Waters, who had been thrown out of UKIP for being too close to the street-fighting wing of fascism – this is niche nationalism.

---

* As a long-term enthusiast for modern music, a socialist and a patron of the Manchester Modernist Society, Marr is guiltless of most of Morrissey's specific crimes.

Going back to *The Smiths* LP, what you can hear in it now is
a total refusal to *get over* and *move on* from a series of childhood
wounds. Sometimes these are Morrissey's own — several songs
are, or appear to be, about gay relationships, frequently with a
stark power differential, as for instance in the brutal awakening
described in 'Reel Around the Fountain'. Sometimes they linger
on murder, with vivid depictions that stand somewhere between
a Tony Harrison poem and a *News of the World* headline. In the
closing song 'Suffer Little Children', over chiming, pretty but
eerily looping guitars, references to the victims of Ian Brady and
Myra Hindley, children of Morrissey's generation murdered on
the wild moors around Greater Manchester, are interspersed with
the landscape:

> fresh lilaced moorland fields
> cannot hide the stolid stench of death.

The way the song's cadences recur and recur, murmured with
grim pleasure, suggests not rage or empathy so much as a taste-
ful version of tabloid prurience, a fascination with horror. The
best-known songs on the record are either depictions of miserable bedsit life ('What do we get for our trouble and pain? Just
a rented room in Whalley Range'), or statements of both identification and opposition to 'England', which is 'mine', and 'it
owes me a living — but ask me why and I'll spit in your eye'. In
this song, 'Still Ill', the poignant nostalgia — and its identification
with the particular environment of a depressed, damp, formerly
industrial city — is unrivalled, all the more for its vagueness, the
indistinct object of its longing:

> But we cannot cling
> to the old dreams anymore
> No we cannot cling
> to those dreams
> Under the iron bridge we kissed
> and although I ended up with sore lips
> it just wasn't like the old days anymore
> No it wasn't like those days.

So sang a man of twenty-three. It would have seemed odd in 1983, when that record came out, to see it as an incipient statement of English nationalism, particularly given that the band seemed in some way identified, albeit in a complex fashion, with the left: playing benefit concerts for Liverpool Council; being proudly queer (although never 'out') in the repressive era that culminated in the passing of Section 28; and particularly in their strange but fervent republicanism, as outlined in the 'The Queen Is Dead', a kaleidoscopic fantasy narrating surreal imagined encounters with Prince Charles and culminating in regicide, though the dream of insurgency is tempered by the song's citation of the wartime music hall number 'Take Me Back to Dear Old Blighty'.

The cruelty of Morrissey's vision would become apparent only gradually. Indeed, many of the Smiths' songs described the victimisation perpetrated by a Victorian industrial elite that somehow endured right into the secondary-modern schools of the 1960s. In 'The Headmaster Ritual', sung in the present tense but describing an experience unlikely to be found in any urban local authority school in the 1980s, we have:

Belligerent ghouls
run Manchester schools
spineless bastards all
Sir leads the troops
jealous of youth
same old jokes since 1902.

'Barbarism Begins at Home', from the same album, paints the same scenario, but in a domestic setting – pointless arbitrary violence, casual and random, again with a sense of endless repetition and inevitability:

And a crack on the head
is what you get for asking
And a crack on the head
is what you get for not asking.

These songs, Derek Jarman's videos for them and the inextricably linked covers of the albums and singles, usually designed or directed by Morrissey himself, exist in an enclosed world that ends around 1964, at an undefined point just before the large-scale migration from the cotton-producing regions of south Asia into the textile-manufacturing districts of the North West of England: before Harold Wilson's election victory, before the Beatles went weird, before inner-Manchester districts like Hulme were subjected to modernist 'comprehensive redevelopment', before the textile industry collapsed, and after the introduction of television but certainly before colour TV, with pop music defined by Joe Meek, Billy Fury and Lulu rather than psychedelia or soul.

The creation and evocation of this pickled environment are remarkably complete, and is achieved with such longing and lingering attention to detail that it can only be seen as an attempt at reconstructing it, in its entirety, in the mind. In this, the Smiths were remarkably successful – though I was born a year before the band was formed, if I hear 'Rusholme Ruffians' I immediately relate it to the casual violence and the wet red Victorian streets of the southern port where I grew up. The thoroughness of the evocation seems to make the pettiness and misery of the memories it calls forth forgivable.

In a 1988 *Melody Maker* interview/feature on Morrissey, timed to coincide with the release of *Viva Hate*, his first, and by far his best, solo record, Simon Reynolds refers to this bleak nostalgia: '*Viva Hate* ... returns again and again to the Englishness which obsesses Morrissey ... [he] seems to cherish the very constraints and despondency of a now disappearing England, [fetishising] the lost limits.' Reynolds tries to corner the singer about this, asking him:

> On 'Late Night, Maudlin Street', you say 'I never stole a happy hour around here' – but the whole effect of the song, the way your murmured reveries drift in and out of Vini [Reilly]'s entranced playing, just makes the whole time and place seem magical, otherworldly, and incredibly precious.

Admitting the charge, Morrissey replies, 'it's a trick of memory ... looking back and thinking maybe things weren't that bad but of course, they were'.*

It first became clear that this all had a certain vicious underside in 1986, when the Smiths released 'Panic', with its attack not so much on chart pop per se, but upon any and all kinds of

---

* Simon Reynolds, 'Miserablism', *Blissed Out: The Raptures of Rock*, London, 1990, pp. 16–17.

black dance music. Around the time of its release, a *New Musical Express* questionnaire asked him to name his 'favourite reggae record'; he replied, 'reggae is vile', and later attempted to justify this response by claiming that the genre is a form of 'black nationalism'. In 'Panic', the detailed picture of miserable British (and in this case, also Irish) urbanism and the lack of consolation in the countryside is paired with the arrival of an inescapable alien force that poisons that environment.

> Hopes may rise on the Grasmere
> But Honey Pie, you're not safe here
> So you run down
> to the safety of the town
> But there's Panic on the streets of Carlisle
> Dublin, Dundee, Humberside
> I wonder to myself
> Burn down the disco
> hang the blessed DJ
> Because the music that they constantly play
> IT SAYS NOTHING TO ME ABOUT MY LIFE.

Viva Hate features the first of several solo Morrissey songs that include uncomfortable depictions of British Asians – 'Bengali in Platforms' patronisingly tells the out-of-place, eager-to-please protagonist, trying to fit in with Anglo-American pop culture, 'life is hard enough when you belong here'. This becomes creepier still with 'Asian Rut', a dispassionate anecdote of a racist attack, and 'National Front Disco', an anthemic portrayal of 1970s English fascists that includes 'England for the English!' as a warbled refrain. When supporting Madness in 1992, Morrissey wrapped himself in a Union Jack at a time when public display of the flag was largely the preserve of the far right; this was seen, at least by the music press, as a gesture towards the group's large skinhead fan base.

The singer's support for the far right has passed well beyond the point of plausible deniability in the last couple of years. In a recent interview on his own website, Morrissey reaffirmed his support for Anne Marie Waters (elsewhere, he has declared his enthusiasm for 'Tommy Robinson'), added that he'd like to see Nigel Farage become prime minister and reiterated his disdain for Islam. He has greeted accusations of racism with the comment 'Everyone ultimately prefers their own race – does this make everyone racist?' On his own Facebook fan page last year, Morrissey denounced 'Soviet Britain'. These are all fairly standard statements of contemporary British conservatism, made strange only by the fact that they come from a queer 1980s pop star who hasn't lived in the UK in decades, rather than a retired Trafford Park engineer.

The most extraordinary achievement of Morrissey's career since 1988 has been getting his 2013 autobiography published by Penguin Classics from day one. The experience of reading it is equally bizarre. It begins with a hundred pages on 1960s Manchester, written with the same obsessive longing that pervades the songs of the Smiths, with the same flair and precision, the same apparent attempt to recreate a complete society in all its misery and violence, a world in microcosm – followed by three hundred interminable pages, tedious and self-important, about celebrities, record companies and court cases, notable only for an air of breathtaking self-pity.

It's tempting simply to separate out these two phases, much as it is to separate the Smiths from the sixty-one-year-old suburban fascist who fronted them. But the two are intrinsically linked. It can be difficult to work out quite what it is about the past that so many in Morrissey's generation long for. It certainly isn't council housing, full employment, free education, public ownership or social mobility: if conservative over-sixties comment on such lost public goods, it's to decry the Labour Party's foolish utopianism in trying to resurrect them. Rather, it is a nostalgia for misery, a longing for boredom, a relocation of poverty from economics to aesthetics.*

The belligerent ghouls. The spineless bastards. The beatings. The ignorance. The pollution and the soot. The gay-bashing and the Paki-bashing. The murders on the Moors. The young are resented for not having suffered these miseries, obsessively recalled so as constantly to relive the experience of personal struggle and uprooting, an origin story for home ownership and bored affluence, whether that's the pettier example of the paid-off mortgage or the purchased council house, or, in Morrissey's case, the villa in the hills of LA. But the young are resented not only for their freedom from the past. Who stands in the way of this self-aggrandisement through re-enactment? The Asians, especially the Muslims. The young. The left. The 'woke'. And here, Morrissey is truly the voice of a generation.

---

* For anyone who doubts this, I recommend browsing the Facebook group 'Memory Lane UK'.

9

If Hopes Were Dupes,
Fears May Be Liars

Rory MacQueen

In the wake of Labour's landslide general election defeat on 9 June 1983, leading lights of the left gathered their thoughts in a *New Socialist* and Polity Press collected volume, *The Future of the Left.*[*] The book fought back against the near-unanimous demand in the mainstream media for a return to the 'middle ground'. It can be read as a message in a bottle, from those who watched the neoliberal era coalesce, to us who are witnessing its elongated crisis, and, if we want to avoid suffering the same disappointments, we must learn from the debates of that time.

Existential questions are today being asked about Labour's viability as an electoral coalition and political project. Successive elections have been lost by the right, centre and left of the Party, though Jeremy Corbyn remains the only Labour leader since Tony Blair to gain seats at a general election. For the neoliberal

---

[*] James Curran, ed., *The Future of the Left*, Cambridge, 1984.

centre, 2019's election manifesto 'It's Time for Real Change' can be portrayed as another 'longest suicide note in history', but the left cannot allow the myth to take hold that socialism was to blame for the latest election fiasco, or that success at the ballot box will follow from the Party ditching the left-most elements of the Corbyn programme.

In 1983, Margaret Thatcher exploited a nationalist opportunity – in place of Brexit, the Falklands – to rout a Labour opposition divided over policy, leadership and reselection. Labour lost sixty seats and the Tories secured a Commons majority of 140. Contributors to *The Future of the Left* agonised over whether Labour would ever be able extend its electoral reach beyond its industrial heartlands. Concern about class dealignment was already evident. Sociologist John Westergaard noted a drop in support for the Party among manual workers, as well as a failure to attract voters in the expanding white-collar and 'white-blouse' groups, but according to Richard Hyman, 'the class basis of party choice' had been weakening for a quarter of a century. Other demographics appeared equally unfavourable for Labour, too. The swing away from Labour 'was more marked amongst first-time voters than amongst other age-groups', observed Philip Cohen, with 42 per cent of eighteen- to twenty-four-year-olds voting Conservative.

What had gone wrong? 'The unpopularity of the left is not so much due to popular disagreement with left ideals (if they've ever heard of them), as to an absence of any apparent strategy for putting them into practice and therefore a feeling that they are pie in the sky', argued Doreen Massey, Lynne Segal and Hilary Wainwright. Tony Benn argued similarly: 'If hope is to replace fear, people have to be able to believe that there is an alternative. Unfortunately for us, the electorate did not believe in Labour's alternative – and wondered whether we all believed in it either.'

Contributors tried to get a handle on the essential character of the Conservative government. Anthony Barnett seemingly misjudged Thatcher as 'more the flotsam left behind on the beach by a retreating post-war tide than she is the tide of history itself'. The prime minister had been 'over-estimated ideologically and under-estimated economically'. Barnett was even clearer than other contributors that a total break from the post-war consensus would be welcome: 'Consensus politics meant restrictive practices writ large, not reform. Its passing should not be lamented.' Realisation was dawning that Thatcher's first term hadn't been a historical blip but rather marked the start of a new political epoch, and some were clearer about how. 'Paradoxically, she does raise hearts and minds an inch or two because, vile, corrupt, awful as her vision of the future is, we *know* what it is,' commented Stuart Hall. 'The one thing nobody knows is what Labour conceives to be an "alternative way of life". It currently possesses no image of the future. It provides no picture of life under socialism.'

David Edgar sketched out distinctions on the Tory right between economic liberals and social authoritarians. The Institute of Economic Affairs and Centre for Policy Studies successfully propagandised for the so-called 'free market', while, on the other hand, philosopher Roger Scruton was hoping that 'sentiments of sovereignty and national honour' stirred by the Falklands War 'would be reflected in domestic policy, such as that relating to immigration and capital punishment'.

Was the answer for the left a 'progressive alliance' with the SDP-Liberal Alliance? Almost every paragraph in Neil Kinnock's offering for *The Future of the Left* contains the words 'liberty' or 'freedom', perhaps with one eye on Alliance voters.

It fell to Raymond Williams to sound a note of warning. His essay examined the potential for both a 'Big Coalition', involving some or all of the Alliance, and a 'Smaller Coalition' consisting of a Labour Party which had set aside disagreements to unite around a minimal centre-left agenda. If either group was united around some generally progressive ideas, he observed, there was little to be lost from coalescing, but none of the potential areas of commonality were 'in any distinctive sense socialist'. If socialists did not believe that moderate Keynesian social democracy was adequate for sustained economic recovery or political advance, then there was little to be gained from a coalition based around it:

> Whether it's the Big or the Smaller version, the advocates of either have in effect abandoned the struggle to transform belief and opinion. In a cold climate, they say, the many but now disparate remnants of decent and sensible opinion must huddle together, pooling their surviving resources against the Tory storm. I can see how easy it is to feel like that or to respond hopefully to a few brave words flung back against the wind ... We can sustain the Smaller Coalition without any real work on policies, or reach out for the Larger Coalition, adapting ahead of its formal arrangements by trimming or underplaying those innovative socialist policies which are known to be incompatible with it. But we can then draw a clear line, to our mutual advantage, between socialists and coalition-ists. We can begin to see where we really are, and what we have to change.

In some ways, the difficulties we face in 2020 are worse than those of the 1980s, with 'heartland' seats lost and little evidence of a realignment elsewhere happening fast enough to compen-sate. Scottish voters returned forty-one Labour MPs in 1983. The miners and printers had not yet been smashed and trade union membership – around double today's level – had only just begun its decline from its historic high.

But the contrasts with 1983 are no less important. Michael Foot had been James Callaghan's deputy and was elected leader on a unity ticket, rather than on a left manifesto from the backbenches. Mike Gapes and Chris Leslie are not Roy Jenkins and Shirley Williams, and Michel Barnier is not General Galtieri. In 2019 the new ideas belonged to Labour, not the Conservatives, but we failed to frame our vision for the country and were trumped by the promise of a Johnson Brexit which won the support of voters for whom 'things were better back in the day'.

Labour's policies last December were popular in themselves but we have been told repeatedly that – echoing Benn in 1983 – voters didn't believe we would, or could, implement them.* Key pledges from 2017 – higher income tax rates for the wealthy, nationalisation of the utilities and free university tuition – were familiar enough to the electorate, but 2019 additions, such as a four-day working week, universal basic income, net-zero emissions and free broadband, required imagination.

This doesn't mean Labour must limit its horizon to what has gone before, but it reminds us that capturing the initiative requires more than just announcing new-sounding things, and that futurism in itself doesn't guarantee greater electoral success than speaking to already existing interests and desires.

For decades, all wings of the party (but especially centrists) have attempted to put some distance between themselves and the 1945–79 period, in an effort to appear modern. For all the

---

* Canvassers also reported many people asking, in one form or another, whether a party that promises to implement a referendum result and then changes its mind is to be trusted to implement the most far-ranging and ambitious restructuring of the British economy in forty years.

political and economic shortcomings of 'welfare capitalism', we have to consider whether the effect of renouncing its era has been to concede a pivotal moment to those on the right who want to claim its most reactionary elements.

While in some respects the outlook is gloomier than it was in 1983, there are chinks of sunlight, and not just in the youthful profile of Labour's vote. Thatcher's reforms successfully kick-started capitalism in the aggregate by redistributing power from labour to capital and unleashing the finance sector. Subsequently, with headline growth and profits healthy, and wages rising for many, New Labour was able to provide better public services and tax credits to prop up earnings for those who weren't benefiting.

But in the post-2008 world, it's unclear whether either Boris Johnson or post-Thatcher Tory 'moderates' have any solution to the economic problems implied by productivity growth of just 0.3 per cent over the last decade. Wage rises must generally come from either increasing productivity or increasing workers' bargaining power: there is no evidence that the Conservatives have an answer to the former, beyond a smattering of capital investment, or that they are willing to countenance the latter. Labour's failure to oust the Tories in 2019 means we are left with a government which, despite having won the political battle, doesn't have a plan to cope with the big economic challenges of our time.

Is Johnson as much of a departure from his Conservative predecessors as Thatcher was? The prime minister may be determined to prosecute a culture war while ditching 'fiscal discipline' but questions remain over how deeply committed his party is to the public spending aspects of his programme, with widespread grumbling in the Tory base about possible tax rises. Four years after Theresa May floated compulsory worker representation on company boards, Johnson's threat to ban public sector strikes and a planned local government settlement that redistributes upwards hardly suggest a straightforwardly leftward shift in economic policy.

Williams's comments about coalition unity between the left and the centre left remain valid. Keir Starmer's commitment to 'common ownership' – as distinct from public ownership – potentially leaves the door open to leaving key utilities in the hands of the few, not the many: perhaps along the lines of Welsh Water, a private non-profit company structure run by opaquely appointed 'members' unaccountable to the public, staff or voters. Crossing our fingers or pleading for unity will not make this political faultline go away.

Others would now like to build a coalition through rotating the left onto the axes of the culture war, taking up Johnson's invitation to a fight on his own terms by lining up with socially liberal centrists. On this basis, the correct observation that the working class is not just northern, white and Leave-voting invites adherence to *anything* that signals distance from that 'old-fashioned' left. The divide ceases to be left–right and becomes open–closed or Remain–Leave, with the last one sharing a liberal distaste for organised labour. Massey, Segal and Wainwright's 'Great-Moving-Right-Male-Left-Show' describes today's ex-Trotskyists and post-capitalists as neatly as the Eric Hobsbawms and others for whom it was coined.

The alternative is not a plea to concede or shut up about 'cultural' issues. Fighting to defend and extend non-economic rights is a necessary but insufficient condition for the left. There will also always be areas of overlap and common interest with those who are not socialists. But even small coalitions must start, as Williams says, from an honest assessment of where we are, not from pretending existing ideological questions have disappeared.

During the years of Peter Mandelson's 'sealed tomb', the Labour left may have hoped that, if only our ideas were heard, they would automatically mean electoral success. If that was wrong, it's clear from 2017 that a shift to the left doesn't automatically lead to electoral annihilation either. The economic problems that burst out into the open in the financial crisis of 2008 have not been tidied neatly away.

If there is one lesson from the defeats of the 1980s, perhaps it ought to be the one from Massey, Segal, Wainwright and Benn: an ambitious programme can only succeed if the Party truly believes in it and knows how it is going to make it a reality. As Corbyn likes to quote from Pablo Neruda, they can cut the flowers but they can't stop spring from coming. We can be forgiven for mistaking snowdrops for daffodils, but we need to learn humbly from our mistakes and those of our predecessors if we are to see where we really are, and what we have to change, and to tend effectively the stirring of socialist thought and activity in the Labour Party, which now exists thanks to those who led, supported and sustained Corbynism while it lasted.

10
Beyond Parliamentary Socialism?
Leo Panitch in Interview

GB: Looking back on December 2019, is there anything you think that Labour could have done differently during the election? Or had the leadership run out of options by that point?

LP: I'm sure Labour could have done various things differently over the course of the election, although I think the die was cast by that point. Although it could have been rolled out differently, I think that the manifesto was a more coherent document this time around than it was in 2017, even though the slogan of 2017 really registered in a way this one didn't. By virtue of being structured around the Green New Deal, the manifesto was both more coherent and more radical. So much of the 2017 Manifesto was oriented towards increasing Britain's competitiveness, which may be necessary in a capitalist world, especially given the nature of the City of London, but it is also very compromised to stress that we need these policies to increase our competitiveness. Framing the manifesto around the Green New

Deal in 2019 actually made it a more coherent radical progressive programme.

That said, I don't think this came across, for reasons that various people have pointed to. James Meadway was right to suggest that, for many Labour voters who had voted Leave, the way each new item was rolled out separately could seem like a series of bribes to look away from being given the finger over how they voted on Brexit. I also think that during the campaign, Jeremy Corbyn's weaknesses became clear. Of course, everything that happened in the run-up to the campaign to undermine his position on Brexit contributed to that – but to watch him being so tongue-tied in his debate with Boris Johnson, you couldn't ever have imagined Tony Benn being as tongue-tied and looking as flummoxed as Jeremy did. Now, one of the attractive things about Jeremy is that he wasn't a retail politician, and he was self-deprecating about that, which was one of his strengths. But by that point, his best weapons had been taken from him over the Brexit question. I think those were the two things during the election campaign that stood out to me as most problematic.

What were the most significant strategic errors and successes of Corbyn's leadership of Labour?

Had Labour been able to stick to its position on Brexit in the 2017 election – and indeed made a virtue of it rather than being ashamed of it – I think the whole situation would have been different. In that sense, it's incredibly ironic that the person in the shadow cabinet who played such a significant role in driving Labour off its 2017 position is about to be elected as leader. That's not to say Keir Starmer caused this – he was merely the conduit of the People's Vote campaign – but in 2017, the Party said, 'the people have voted, this is an exercise in democracy, we have to accept it.' You can go through the list of quotes from senior Labour politicians saying just this. But when the polls started showing that Remain might win a second referendum, and Peter Mandelson put his evil hand in, what happened was that, as always, the Labour left took the responsibility for Party unity on its shoulders.

Once Chuka Umunna and the independents got the wind in their sails, it looks to me like Corbyn got frightened that many more would follow, so he gave in to the second referendum appeal. I think that was disastrous. Now, it's true this was a very difficult situation, and one can argue that many Labour voters elsewhere would have gone over to the Lib Dems – one can never know. But what we do know is that this was the worst outcome possible, so it would have been better to have gone with the other one.

It now looks to me like it would have been best for the Corbyn leadership to have agreed to Theresa May's deal. I don't know that this could have been done, what with May constantly bleating about how Brexit means Brexit, while offering the Europeans very soft arrangements. But in that moment when May did have the cross-party talks, it probably would have been best for the Corbyn leadership to have agreed to May's deal, leaving the Tories divided. Labour would have been divided too, but the Tories even more. Of course, this is easy for me to say, and there were various moments during the winter when I felt that Labour simply wasn't being heard in the debate in the media, and they might as well go for the second referendum. So, it's easy to say all this now, but in retrospect I think the changed position over Europe was one major strategic error.

What about the wider left? What have been the strategic successes and failures of Momentum, the unions and the various social movements that have been part of the Corbyn project?

What was triggered by Corbyn's leadership campaign was remarkable, and I'm not sure how much more could have been achieved given the nature of the Labour Party. The majority of the Parliamentary Party are not socialists – they genuinely believe that we should get along within capitalism as best we can. Given the nature of the Party apparatus and the mostly depoliticised nature of the union membership, what was achieved by Momentum, The World Transformed [TWT], Novara was remarkable. Of course, I wish that Momentum had played a much more active role in political education. I wish that, above all, [Len] McCluskey and [Ian] Murray at Unite could have found a way to construct an equivalent to Momentum inside their union. I think Murray certainly was inclined to, but it's a very difficult thing to do. However much one does want to say that not nearly enough was done, the achievements were truly extraordinary.

In the book that Colin Leys and I have just finished, the penultimate chapter, written long before the election was called, ends with a quote from Ben Sellers, from 2018:

> If you'd asked me five years ago what the plan was, I would have said: build locally in CLPs, win policy arguments, organise at conference; get more representative MPs; win the leadership – in that order. I would have talked in terms of a 10-year plan at a minimum. Instead, we did it back to front, winning the leadership in an extraordinary summer. None of that gave us time to educate, organise and agitate in the rest of the party and movement.

I also felt back in the seventies, however admirable the CLPD [Campaign for Labour Party Democracy] and the Bennite decade-long attempt to democratise the Party in the way they hoped to was, and I did admire it enormously, that it would not be successful. This was because I always knew that it would split the Labour Party, and that since divided parties cannot win the election, it would be the left which would take party unity on its shoulders as the expense of giving up on the Party's transformation.

This is not to deny the critical importance of having a democratised socialist party if you're going to democratise the state. But so far, this has largely been impossible. My generation failed to create those kinds of mass democratic socialist parties outside the old social-democratic parties. So in that context, it is not surprising that the effort has bubbled up again inside the Labour Party. What is more amazing is that it simultaneously bubbled up inside the Democratic Party in the US. And in those places where you had proportional representation, a real realignment took place with the creation of new parties like Die Linke, Syriza, Podemos, etc. Of course, they're all now in alliances with social-democratic parties at national or regional levels, so one really can't say that the track that the British new left embarked on with Corbyn is to be dismissed after this defeat.

In a recent interview with Tribune, *you say, 'The lesson is that it's very difficult to transform these parties. But there are encouraging signs — the size of Momentum, the role of left-wing unions in supporting Corbynism. There is a lot to be said for fighting to continue the effort in the coming years.' What are the grounds for thinking this will be more successful this time?*

It all depends on whether the left can build a stronger base, and it's not clear that they can – particularly when it comes to political education. However impressive TWT and Momentum are, it's clear that a significant number of people who were mobilised to join the Labour Party as a result of Corbyn's leadership were ready to vote for Starmer. The fact that so few of them joined through their constituency Labour Parties, and many never attended a CLP meeting, tells us a great deal about the gaps that exist in organising and mobilising this group. It is true that Momentum had many more people involved – including at CLP level – than the CLPD ever did. But one could see that there wasn't much political education going on in the CLPs, so the base wasn't being created for what Corbyn was attempting to do.

What is now needed is for activists to get involved in their CLPs – however deadly boring going to their meetings may be initially – and really turn them into something most of them have never been: interesting centres of working-class life. There's no sense pretending that most CLPs have ever been that. The other issue is changing the nature of union branches. It has always been clear that if you're really going to change the Labour Party, you need to change at least a core number of unions – and I don't just mean change them at the top.

At that point, one can think about making changes to the Party apparatus – expanding and deepening the campaign team, choosing new regional organisers, etc. Should all this happen, much of the centre-right of the party would still eventually split but the left would come away with the Party apparatus and with the bulk of the union ties. You would then have a very different Labour Party. I'm not optimistic that this will happen, but I don't see any other way forward.

In that same interview, you say, 'Every time there has been this attempt to transform the Labour Party — and it has happened many times — it has been the result of a great crisis of capitalism.' Do you think we are entering such a moment now?

Corbyn emerged, belatedly, out of the crisis of 2008 and the subsequent political crisis created by austerity, which delegitimated neoliberalism — though to the benefit of UKIP as much as the left. This current moment of crisis associated with the pandemic is different in that it doesn't have its roots in the contradictions of the economic system. When I gave that quote, I was thinking of 1929–31, when [George] Lansbury — the socialist pacifist — emerged as leader of the Labour Party. I was thinking of the 1970s crisis of stagflation when the Bennite[s] emerged, and I was thinking of the 2008 crisis. This is a crisis of a very different kind. I think if I had to make a parallel, it would be the moment Lansbury was displaced in 1935, when the Labour Party endorsed rearmament and Clement Attlee took over. As Ralph Miliband put it in his book *Parliamentary Socialism*, it was at this point that a much 'more responsible team' took over leadership of the Labour Party, which was elected in 1945. The 1945 Labour government was certainly influenced by the radicalism produced by the crisis of 1931 and the sharp shift to the left in Labour Party policy that followed. The way things are going now, I think we might see that type of 'more responsible team' emerging. So, I think that's the more likely parallel.

What should the left expect from Starmer? Expulsions and attempts to de-democratise the party, or a reconciliation with Corbynism?

I doubt we'll see mass expulsions, at least not for as long as McCluskey is head of Unite. That said, I think this insidious antisemitism campaign is very much mixed up with an anti-socialist animus and could be used as a lever for trying to get part of the left out. But since most left activists aren't primarily motivated by the issue of Israel – however justified it is to criticise the Israeli government's policies – this can only go so far. With Starmer, I think we will see the kind of politics that the new Tribune group inside the PLP, formed just a year or so ago, represents. It is a very broad-based group of the centre left, extending to the centre right, and it will look to reviving a politics of compromise. Of course, one needs to compromise strategically all the time; that's fine provided one understands what one is doing. But compromising for the sake of compromise with no strategic orientation, especially now we have a unified Tory party, only creates ideological confusion.

The 2008 financial crisis and its effects changed Labour Party policy in quite important ways, and I don't think that will be easily undone. There won't be much reason to undo it given the nature of the contemporary crisis – by which I mean ecological as well as economic, and political for that matter, given the state's incapacity to cope with the epidemic as well as the ecological crisis. So I don't think we will see a return to Blairism. And I think even Joe Biden will have to take on board a lot of the policies Bernie Sanders has been advocating in the US. So I don't think it is all going to be undone, but Starmer will put the agenda forward in a way that is rather anodyne and without conviction.

What about socialist movements in the rest of the world – do you see any signs of hope now it looks as though the Corbyn/Sanders moment is over?

We're in for the long haul. We should have said this all along. As Marx told the insurrectionists in 1851, we're involved in a ten, fifteen, twenty-year process – he really should have said 150–200 years! I realise that runs against the time horizon posed by the ecological crisis, but any proposed solution to that crisis is implausible without building up the necessary political capacity; the degree of planning and collective consciousness involved that needs to be built for an adequate response to the climate crisis is huge. We have to understand that Jeremy was a short-cut, Sanders was a shortcut. But after two decades of protesting against neoliberalism, and after Occupy, these were shortcuts that were based on the recognition that you can protest for ever and the world won't change. The disappointment of Syriza, of the Corbyn project, and now the movement behind Sanders too, is palpable. But at least it will show people that they need to be putting their shoulders to the wheel for the long haul.

But all the things that they have built – Momentum, the DSA [Democratic Socialists of America], *Jacobin*, The World Transformed, the new *Tribune* magazine – now need to be used to develop circles of socialist activists at every level. They can be engaged in electoral politics, but they can't only be engaged in electoral politics. In the case of the Labour Party – because there's a real party structure, and many of the largest unions are sympathetic to this approach – there's much more of a basis for doing this than inside the Democratic Party, because it is simply an electoral network with no real structural apparatus. While DSA activists will still, and very rightly so, mobilise to try to get socialists on the democratic electoral tickets in electoral contests, ranging from local dog catchers to state senators, I am not sure the DSA has the capacity or the clarity to undertake extensive political education. Only the Bread and Roses Coalition within the DSA understand that what they have been engaged in really is a process of class formation, and that further engagement with electoral politics should be oriented to aiding that project. Others think that it is still possible to transform the Democratic Party but to some extent they are fostering an illusion. So I fear that the best people involved in the DSA will take various different tacks after the election.

Yet I still feel more optimistic than I have for a very long time about the prospects of this long-run struggle, because so many people have come on board. The numbers – even if the core activists are only around the five or ten thousand mark in the DSA and Momentum – are phenomenal, and these activists can become remarkable organisers as well as educators. I'm not dismayed precisely because I never thought this was going be easy.

What do you imagine the ruling class response to the current coronavirus crisis will be? It looks like we're going to see a significant expansion in the size of the state, but obviously catered to the interests of capital and the Tory electoral base. How should the left respond to this?

The situation is very frightening – we are at a truly terrible moment in human history – but there are also some positive things that can be – and are being – learned from it. On the cultural/ideological level people are recognising that we can't all be in it for ourselves – that this is a collective problem and only collective solutions will do. But deeper than this, we are now seeing governments all around the world adopting the policies that we have been arguing for. All over the world, states are undertaking massive deficit spending at levels that would shock even the modern monetary theory theorists. The size of the deficits is staggering. We can more readily now say, 'Look at what Corbyn could have done – don't Corbyn's fiscal policies now look quite rational? Indeed, don't they look small in relation to this?'

But we must admit that this can work because every state in the world is doing it – that is where the MMT theorists were wrong. Usually, what the bond traders are looking at are the spreads – what is the size of the Italian deficit compared to the German one. Insofar as deficits are exploding everywhere, the disciplining effect of the bond vigilantes is less powerful. Now, in a sense, this disciplining effect never exists for the US. The US deficit was already through the roof, it's now going through the stratosphere. And the world is still rushing to get US dollars because it's the one store of value in the world economy. This crisis is demonstrating that the argument Sam Gindin and I put forward about the internationalisation of the US state – that is, it being the state of global capitalism – is correct. The US state is the protector of capital at a global level, and property owners all over the world look to the US state as their protector, even as they wonder whether or not the US state can play that role.

Of course once the crisis ebbs, the arbitrage will begin again, assuming that bond markets are reconstructed the way they were. Yet I still think there is something we can take strategically out of this that really should give us a lot of solace and encouragement. The fact that Labour was elected in 1945 after the Second World War made it so clear that those who said 'it can't be done' in 1931 were wrong. I think it's going to be possible to make that argument in the coming years about the policies Corbyn and John McDonnell were advocating before this crisis. With every state on a wartime footing, it really allows us to make the case for planning; it really allows us to make the case, and even much better than Labour did in 1945, that the way the state is structured is inadequate for the type of planning needed for the challenges we face today.

We need to be making the case now – not for breaking up the banks, which is absurd – but for using this crisis to take them over. We must make the case for taking over the banks that need to be saved, as the Swedes did in the early nineties, but not to give them back as the Swedes did. We need to make the case that turning the banking system into a public utility is essential for the planning necessary for the Green New Deal. Whatever the state does to turn manufacturing firms towards the production of ventilators must become an example for why and how we can require existing industries to engage in conversion more generally. Even if this doesn't involve nationalisation, we can make the case for the types of measures that were introduced during the war, when CEOs were brought in, made state employees, and told to convert auto production into airplane production. And given the collapse of oil prices and of the oil company stocks, we can make the case that the state should be buying them out with bare minimum compensation to the end of effecting the transition to the production of clean energy. So, there's a lot that we can build out of this, and the fact that we had started to make the case for many of these policies before the crisis means we have a lot to build on.

How do you think we will look back on this political moment – the period between the last crash and the coming one?

I would like us to look back on this moment as the point at which we saw the emergence of a politicised generation. That is a remarkable development. A generation of young politicised people has emerged out of the denigration of the socialist ambition by so much of the left – not just by the Kinnockites, the Blairites and the Clintonites, of course, but also the postmodernist left, the identity politics left. So, to see this generation emerge is remarkable and that's what we need to build on.

Of course, currently the project is more ambitious than it is strategically well founded, but the strategic instincts of this new generation are admirable. They know that we need to get into the state and change it somehow. There's loads that needs to be done in terms of developing organising capacities: it isn't just a matter of reading *Jacobin* or *Tribune* or listening to Novara, they must learn how to organise working people. That involves real skills and real commitment and a tremendous amount of patience, as well as a willingness to be able to sacrifice a lot. Easy for old Marxist professors in universities to say, I know, but I so think this is the new generation's greatest challenge.

II. FUTURES

11

The Coronavirus and the Crisis this Time

Sam Gindin

So many out-of-the way things had happened lately, that Alice has begun to think that very few things indeed were really impossible.

Lewis Carroll, *Alice's Adventures in Wonderland*

Crises – not regular downturns but *major* crises – are characterised by the uncertainty they bring. In the midst of these periodic calamities, we don't know how or even whether we will stumble out of them, or what to expect if they do end. Crises are consequently moments of turmoil with openings for new political developments, good and bad.

Because each such crisis modifies the trajectory of history, the subsequent crisis occurs in a changed context and so has its own distinct features. The crisis of the 1970s, for example, involved a militant working class and a challenge to the US dollar; it brought a qualitative acceleration in the role of finance and of globalisation. The crisis of 2008–9, on the other hand, involved a largely defeated working class, confirmed the global supremacy of the dollar and generalised new ways of managing a uniquely finance-dependent economy. Though – like the previous crisis – it yielded more neoliberal financialisation, this time the upheaval, occurring alongside an acute disorientation of traditional political parties, opened the doors to both right-wing and left/centre-left parties.

This crisis is unique in an especially topsy-turvy way. The world, as Alice would say, is getting 'curiouser and curiouser'. In past capitalist crises, the state intervened to try and get the economy going again. This time, states' immediate focus was not how to *revive* the economy, but how to *restrict* it further. In introducing the language of 'social distancing' and 'self-quarantine' to cope with the emergency, governments suspended the social interactions that constitute a good part of the world of work and consumption.

This accent on the social, while putting the economic on the backburner, has brought a rather remarkable reversal in political discourse. A few short months before the pandemic the leader of France was the darling of business everywhere for spearheading the charge decisively to weaken the welfare state. Today Emmanuel Macron is gravely proclaiming that 'free health care … and our welfare state are precious resources, indispensable advantages when destiny strikes'.

Macron was not alone in scrambling into reverse. Politicians of all stripes imposed measures to limit factory production to socially necessary products like ventilators, hospital beds, protective masks and gloves. Governments telling corporations what to produce became commonplace, with the UK's Conservative prime minister, Boris Johnson, calling on auto companies to 'switch from building cars to ventilators', while President

Donald Trump astonishingly went further by 'ordering' General Motors to make ventilators under the Defense Production Act.

At the same time, the crisis has graphically exposed the extreme fragility of working-class budgets. With so many people facing severe deprivation and the threat of social chaos, all levels of government are being pressed to address people's basic health and survival needs. Republicans are now joining Democrats in proposing legislation to postpone mortgage payments, tighten rent controls and cancel interest payments on student debt. Their disagreements are generally not over *whether* to get more money to workers forced to stay at home, and to improve sick pay and unemployment insurance, but *how significant* these supports should be.

This is not to say that the 'economic' is being ignored, only that its traditional precedence is taking a back seat to the social, i.e. the health threat. There remains a deep concern to preserve enough of the economic infrastructure (production, services, trade, finance) to facilitate a return to some semblance of normality 'later'. This is leading to massive bailouts, and this time – unlike the crisis of 2008–9 – the money is flowing not just to banks but also to the consumer services sector, including air travel companies, hotels and restaurants, and in particular to small and medium-sized businesses.

Governments everywhere have, as if by magic, found a way to pay for all kinds of programmes and supports that were previously written off as impossible. But – leaving aside the crucial issue of whether, after years of cutbacks in funds and skills, states have the capacity to carry out such plans fully (or even to effectively distribute funds) – can this all really be paid for simply by printing money?

The common critique is that, in economies at or near full

employment, such massive injections of funds will be inflationary. But given the current reality of record idle capacity, this
concern can be ignored (though there will be bottlenecks and
possible inflation in certain sectors). And with every country
being forced to take the same actions by the pandemic, the usual
discipline of capital outflows is less binding: there are few places
left to run to. Yet contradictions there are, albeit that they take a
different form in our present circumstances.

First, there is in fact no free lunch. After the crisis is over,
the emergency expenditures will have to be paid for. Once the
economy is again operating at full tilt, meeting newly raised
working-class expectations will no longer be possible through
reviving the money presses. There are limited supplies of labour
and natural resources, and choices will have to be made over who
gets what; questions of inequality and redistribution will, given
the history before and during the crisis, be intensified.

Second, as the crisis begins to fade, this rebalancing will happen unevenly. So the flow of capital may restart and, if it flows
out of the countries still suffering, this will raise large questions
about the morality of capital flows. The assumption that financial markets are untouchable may no longer hold: people may
perhaps come to think, like Alice, that 'very few things indeed
[are] really impossible'. To the rebellion against the extent of
inequality might be added a backlash calling for capital controls.

It's true that the global status of the US dollar allows for a
degree of American exceptionalism. In times of uncertainty there
is generally an increased clamour for the dollar. But here too
there is a limit. For one, the consequent rise in the US exchange
rate can make US goods less competitive and further suppress
manufacturing. But more important, international confidence
in the dollar has rested not only on the strength of US financial

markets but also on the US as a safe haven with an economically and politically pliant working class. If that working class were to rebel, the dollar's special status would be compromised.

Openings to the left?

In such uncertain and anxious times, what most people likely crave is a quick return to normality, even if that would entail no shortage of great frustrations. Such inclinations come with a deference to authority to lead us through the calamity, something that has raised concerns about a new wave of state authoritarianism.

We should of course never underestimate the dangers from the right. But the contours of this crisis suggest a different possibility: a predisposition rather for greater openings and opportunities for the political *left*. Underlying the examples noted above is the reality that, at least for now, markets have been sidelined. The urgency over how we allocate labour, resources and equipment has overwhelmed considerations about competitiveness and maximising private profits, reorienting government priorities to focus instead on what is socially essential.

Moreover, as the financial system heads into uncharted territory again and looks to another boundless bailout from central banks and the state, a population watching history exasperatingly repeat itself may not remain as passive as it did a dozen years ago. People will no doubt again reluctantly accept their immediate obligation to save the banks, but politicians cannot help but worry about a popular backlash if this time there is no effective quid pro quo forced on the bankers.

And as well, a cultural change – still too indistinct to assess – may be afoot. The nature of the crisis and the social restrictions essential to overcoming it have made mutuality and solidarity – against individualism and neoliberal greed – the order of the day. An indelible image of this crisis sees quarantined yet inventive Italians, Spaniards and Portuguese congregating on their balconies, to sing, cheer and clap collective tributes to the courage of the health workers doing the most essential work on the front lines of the global war against the coronavirus, often for poverty wages.

All this opens up the prospect – but only the prospect – of a reorientation in social outlooks, as the crisis, and the state responses to it, unfold. What was once taken for granted as 'natural' may now be vulnerable to larger questions about how we *should* live and relate. For economic and political elites this clearly has its dangers. The trick, for them, is to make sure actions that are currently unavoidable are limited in scope and duration. Once the crisis is comfortably over, uncomfortable ideas and chancy measures must be put back in their box and the lid firmly shut. For popular forces, on the other hand, the challenge lies in keeping that box open.

The most obvious ideological shift brought on by the crisis has been in attitudes to healthcare. Opposition in the US to single-payer healthcare today looks all the more outlandish. Elsewhere, those tolerating healthcare for all but determined to impose cuts that left their systems far overstretched – along with those seeing healthcare as another commodity to be administered by emulating business practices rooted in profitability – are in awkward retreat. Their strategy has been exposed as having left us dangerously unprepared to deal with emergencies.

As we look to consolidate this new mood, we should not be content with the defensive game. This is a moment to think more ambitiously and insist on a far more comprehensive notion of what healthcare encompasses. This ranges across longstanding demands for public dental, drug and eye-care services. It raises the adequacy of long-term care facilities, particularly those that are private, but also those in public hands. It poses questions about the exclusion of personal care workers – who care for the sick, disabled and old – from the public health system, and accordingly from unions and safeguards. And, especially given the shortages of essential equipment we now confront, it poses the question of whether the entire chain of healthcare provision, including the manufacture of health equipment, should be in the public domain.

Thinking bigger extends to the connection between food and health, including restoring hot lunches in the school system; it extends to housing policy, and the contradiction of calling for social distancing given the persistence of crowded homeless shelters; it extends to making permanent the temporary sick days now on offer, and to the provision of childcare. It extends as well to taking 'universality' seriously enough to include the migrants who work our fields and the refugees who have been forced out of their communities.

The existential need for antidotes to avoid pandemics places a special responsibility on global drug companies. They have failed us. Bill Gates, the co-founder of Microsoft and no stranger to financial decision making, explained this failure in accounting terms, stating that pandemic products were not being developed because they are 'extraordinarily high-risk investments'– a polite way of saying that corporations won't adequately address the investments involved without massive government funding. The historian Adam Tooze put this more directly: when it comes to pharmaceutical companies prioritising the social over the profitable, 'obscure coronaviruses don't get the same attention as erectile dysfunction'.

The point is that the provision of medicines and vaccines is too important to leave to private companies with their private priorities. Since Big Pharma will only do the research on dangerous future vaccines if governments take the risk, subsidise and coordinate the distribution of the drugs and vaccines, an obvious question arises. Why don't we cut out the self-serving middleman? Why not place all this directly in the hands of the public as part of an integrated healthcare system?

The pandemic next time: the looming environmental catastrophe

The lack of preparedness for the coronavirus sends the clearest warning about the looming environmental crisis. As with this crisis, the longer we wait to address it, the more catastrophic it will be. But unlike the coronavirus, the environmental crisis is not only about ending a temporary health crisis, but about fixing the damage *already done*. As such, it demands transforming everything about how we live, work, travel, play and relate to each other. This will require maintaining and developing the productive capacities to carry out the necessary changes in our infrastructure, homes, factories and offices.

As conventional as the idea of conversion to renewable energy is now becoming, it *is* in fact a radical idea. The well-meaning slogan of a 'just transition' sounds reassuring but falls short. Those it is intended to win over understandably ask, 'Who pays?' The point is that restructuring the economy and prioritising the environment can't happen without comprehensive planning. Such planning implies a challenge to the private property rights that corporations now enjoy.

At the very least, a National Conversion Agency should be

established, with a mandate to ban the closing of facilities that could be recommissioned to serve environmental (and health) needs and to oversee that process. Workers could call on that agency to intervene if they think their workplace is preparing to make mass redundancies. The existence of such an institution would encourage workers to occupy closed workplaces as more than an act of protest; rather than appealing to a corporation that is no longer interested in the facility, their actions could ensure that the agency carries out its mandate.

Such a national agency would have to be supported by regional tech-conversion centres, employing hundreds if not thousands of young engineers enthusiastic to use their skills to address the existential challenge of the environment. Locally elected environmental boards would monitor community conditions, while locally elected job development boards would link community and environmental needs to jobs, workplace conversions and developing worker and plant capacities – all funded federally as part of a *national* plan, and all rooted in active neighbourhood committees and workplace committees.

The banks: once bitten, twice shy

Everything we hope to do in the way of significant change relies upon our ability to confront the dominance of private financial institutions over our lives. The financial system has all the hallmarks of a public utility: it greases the wheels of the economy, both production and consumption, mediates government policy and receives government funding whenever it finds itself in trouble. We currently have neither the political power nor the technical capacity to take control of finance and repurpose it. The challenge, therefore, is twofold. First, we must place the question on the public agenda – if we do not discuss it now, the moment will never be ripe for raising it. Second, we need to carve out specific spaces within the financial system both to achieve particular priorities and to develop the knowledge and skills for eventually running the financial system in our own interests.

A logical starting place is to establish two distinct government-owned banks: one to finance the infrastructural and housing demands that have been so badly neglected; the other to finance the Green New Deal and conversion. If these banks have to compete to get funds and earn the returns to pay off their loans, little will change. The commitment to establish these banks would have to include, as Scott Aquanno argues in a forthcoming paper, politically determined infusions of cash to make the kind of investments that private banks are reluctant to try: financing projects which have a high, if risky social return and low profits by conventional measures. That initial funding could come from a levy on all financial institutions – payback for the massive bail-outs they received from the state.

Democratic planning: an oxymoron?

When the left speaks of democratic planning it is referencing a new kind of state – one that expresses the public will, encourages the widest popular involvement and actively develops the popular capacity to participate, as opposed to reducing people to commodified workers, data points or passive citizens.

'Planning' seems an inoffensive notion in itself: households plan, corporations plan and even neoliberal states plan. But introducing the kind of *extensive* planning we are proposing here calls forth familiar misgivings, fears and antagonisms. These cannot be dismissed by simply blaming corporate and media bias or the legacy of Cold War propaganda. The prejudices of powerful states have a material basis not only in failed experiments elsewhere, but also in their relations with socialist nations that may indeed be bureaucratic, arbitrary, wasteful and inflexible.

Adding the adjective 'democratic' doesn't solve this dilemma. And though international examples may include suggestive policies and structures, the sober truth is that there are no fully convincing models on offer. This leaves us tirelessly repeating our critiques of capitalism – yet, essential as this is, it is not enough.

What we *can* do is start with an unambiguous commitment to assure others that we are not advocating an all-powerful state and that we value the liberal freedoms won historically: the expansion of the vote to all adults, free speech, the right to assembly, protection against arbitrary arrest, state transparency. We should insist that taking these principles seriously demands an extensive redistribution of income and wealth, so that everyone, in substance not just in formal status, has an equal chance to participate.

In emphasising the democratic side of planning, it is absolutely crucial to address specific mechanisms and institutions as a way to facilitate new levels of popular participation. These would include new central capacities, as well as a range of *decentralised* planning bodies such as those referenced earlier: regional research centres, locally elected environmental and job development boards, workplace and neighbourhood committees and sectoral councils.

The health crisis has notably highlighted the necessity for workplace control by those who do the work. Provisions to promote worker autonomy should extend to workers using their direct knowledge to act as guardians of the public interest, and where necessary to act as whistleblowers, under protection of their unions, to expose shortcuts and 'savings' that affect product and service safety and quality.

Unions have of late come more widely to appreciate the importance of getting the public on side for support towards winning their collective bargaining battles.

But something more is needed: a step towards unions formally linking up with the public in broader *political* demands. This could, for example, mean fighting within the state, to establish joint worker–community councils to monitor and modify strategies on an ongoing basis. In the private sector, it could mean workplace conversion committees and workplace sectoral councils presenting their own plans for a just transition.

Three points are critical here. First, widespread worker participation demands widespread unionisation. Second, such local and sectoral participation cannot be developed and sustained without involving and transforming subnational government, to link national and local planning. Third, it is not only subnational institutions that must be transformed but working-class organisations as well. This calls not just for 'better' unions, but for different and more politicised ones.

Conclusion: organising the class

A particularly important development over the past decade has been the shift from protest to politics: the recognition by popular movements of the limits of protest and the consequent need to address electoral power and the state. Yet we are continuing to struggle with *what kind of politics* can transform society. In spite of the impressive space created by Jeremy Corbyn and Bernie Sanders via their work within established parties, both have run into the limits of these parties. The great political danger is that, having come this far and been disappointed, and with no clear political home, the combination of individual exhaustion, collective demoralisation and divisions on where to go next may lead to the dissipation of what was so optimistically developing.

Bravado declarations of capitalism's imminent collapse will not take us very far. They may be popular in some quarters, but they not only exaggerate the inevitability of capitalism's approaching breakdown, but obscure the necessary work of engaging in the long, hard, indefinite battle to change the world. It is one thing to draw hope from the profound crisis capitalism is experiencing, and from capitalism's ongoing insanities. But the key crisis we must focus on is the *internal* one, the one faced by the left itself. In this particular moment the following four elements – focused on the US but with possible wider application – seem fundamental to sustaining and building a relevant left politics.

1. Defend workers through the present crisis

Directly addressing the immediate needs of working people is a basic starting point, especially given the present emergency. In the US, Sanders's 'Emergency Response to the Coronavirus Pandemic' is a valuable resource in this regard, even if it doesn't go as far in a socialist direction as Doug Henwood does.[*]

2. Build/sustain institutional capacities

In the absence of a left political party in the US, and with Sanders's electoral possibilities having faded, the issue for the

---

[*] Doug Henwood, 'Now Is the Time to Fundamentally Transform America', *Jacobin*, 21 March 2020.

left that has operated within the Democratic Party is how to maintain some institutional independence from the party establishment. The only foreseeable strategy is to choose two to three national campaigns and focus on them. The environment might be one, and the fight for universal healthcare seems a logical second choice. The third might be labour law reform, given its importance to altering the balance of class power in America.

3. Make socialists

The Sanders campaign demonstrated a surprising potential for raising funds and recruiting tens of thousands of committed activists. We need to introduce schools that create socialist cadres who can link analytical and strategical thought with learning how to motivate and organise unconvinced workers, and play a role, as socialists did in the 1930s, not just in defending unions but also in transforming them. The campaigns, schools, study groups, public forums, news magazines and journals (such as *Jacobin* and *Catalyst*) would all be infrastructural elements of a possible future left party.

4. Organise the class

Andrew Murray, chief of staff at Unite, has noted the difference between a left that is 'focused' on the working class and one that is 'rooted' in it. The greatest weakness of the socialist left is its limited embeddedness in unions and working-class communities. Only if the left can overcome this gap – which is a cultural gap as much as a political one – is there any possibility of supporting the development of a coherent, confident and independently defiant working class with the capacity and vision to fundamentally challenge capitalism.

12

Anti-Racism Requires More Than Passive Sympathy

Joshua Virasami

'To be neutral, to be passive in a situation,' the historian Howard Zinn tells us, 'is to collaborate with whatever is going on.' If the history of black political struggle in the US – something Zinn, a white ex-soldier, actively participated in – teaches us one thing, it is that meaningful political change happens not just when black and brown people take a stand against racism, but when the wider society moves from being neutral to becoming actively anti-racist.

The Student Nonviolent Coordinating Committee (SNCC) was one of the most formidable organisations in the fight for civil rights. It understood that change occurs when people are moved to action. Students in northern US universities, although sympathetic to the plight of black southerners, remained passive supporters, so the SNCC organised 'freedom buses' for students to come and act as observers. These students witnessed lynchings, attack dogs mauling protestors and fire hoses dislocating bones, and they were transformed into active anti-racists. Enraged by what they had witnessed, these students wrote home to their parents, often passive opponents of the 'riotous' civil rights protestors. On hearing of the injustices first-hand and in their children's voices, many thousands became aligned to the cause, and the entire political climate shifted in relation to the demands of southern freedom movements.

In the wake of the death of George Floyd, we have statements of solidarity from politicians, corporations and even police forces, but these are mere gestures. To be anti-racist means to involve yourself directly in the movement to end racism: to take action. The first step towards becoming an anti-racist is reckoning with the fact that racism is systemic. As the scholar and activist Angela Davis remarks: 'There is an unbroken line of police violence in the US that takes us all the way back to the days of slavery.' Race, as the Australian scholar Patrick Wolfe puts it, is a 'trace of history', a tradition travelling through several hundred years and in part facilitating the birthing of the global North and global South.

The categorisations of race facilitated colonial conquests, enslavement and exploitative labour regimes – all engines of capitalism. Today, the political-economic set-up of the global economy rests on the availability of a cheap, informal labour force, imperialist warfare, extractivism, the mass incarceration of racialised people and mind-blowing inequalities in educational attainment, wages, housing and healthcare. This deep entanglement of accumulation, dispossession and violence is what is meant by the term 'racial capitalism'. For example, in 2016 the Byron burger chain was happily employing migrant staff, some of whom worked fifty hours a week on minimum wage, until it facilitated a Home Office raid to have them deported. Staff reported that Byron entrapped them in a fake meeting-cum-sting operation. Racism and capitalism are inseparable.

For these reasons, nearly all anti-racist mass movements worth their salt have recited tirelessly: ending racism, root and branch, would mean ending a global economic order predicated upon it. Anti-racism is anti-capitalist, and vice versa. There are no two ways around it. An anti-racist must demand a complete rejection of business as usual. An end to racism requires transformation of the global political-economic set-up. This would mean paying workers fair wages across supply chains and ending the ethnicity pay gap, which flies in the face of the primary corporate objective of profit.

So how can you go from being a passive non-racist to an active anti-racist? Anti-racism is the fight to build a mass-participation movement in the workplace, the street and the community. Beyond a protest, a donation, a social media post and a difficult conversation, there's work to be done in tackling the many day-to-day issues underscored by racism. Learning is an essential part of this journey, so make a reading/listening/watching list and include the autobiography of Assata Shakur, of Malcolm X, of Claudia Jones, of Rosa Luxemburg, of Audre Lorde. Explore not just the imperial legacy of Britain and the US, but also the leaders who fought back, from Maurice Bishop to Amilcar Cabral to Thomas Sankara.

To tackle racism, it is necessary to effect material changes in the lives of poor black and brown people. Material changes require us to make movements from moments: this is a huge political moment; now we must build a huge political movement. We must all become anti-racist activists, black, white, brown – all of us. As activists we need to work together, outside the state agencies, which are some of the principal purveyors of systemic racism, to meet the needs of black and brown communities in Britain.

Black and brown people are four times more likely to die from COVID-19 than white people. Being an anti-racist activist means first of all taking up the fight for improved healthcare provision and protective work equipment in these communities. Black and brown people are massively overrepresented in COVID-related searches, arrests and fines. To be an anti-racist means to fight against the sweeping new range of policing powers being used disproportionately against working-class racialised communities.

Criminalisation, gentrification, the 'hostile environment', the closing of local public services: these are all arenas of anti-racist activism. So, find your local anti-racist organisation; if it doesn't exist then set it up. Every youth club, every school staying under the local authority, every saved estate, every anti-deportation and anti-raids group, every local police-monitoring group – all will make concrete differences in improving the lives of racialised communities. When enough of these groups exist, are connected and can show solidarity with one another across cities and towns, then, and only then, will we begin to make inroads into tackling systemic racism.

13

Between Movement and Party:
The Case of Podemos

Cristina Flesher Fominaya

On 13 January 2020, one month after Jeremy Corbyn's Labour Party was routed at the polls, left coalition party Unidas Podemos (UP) entered government in Spain as junior partner to the centre-left PSOE (Partido Socialista Obrero Español, or Spanish Socialist Workers' Party). What lessons can British socialists draw from its experience?

The differences between the two cases shouldn't be underestimated. Labour is one of the UK's traditional parties of government, with a century of accumulated history behind it; Podemos has gone from upstart challenger hybrid party to ministerial officeholder in the space of just six years. But if there are any lessons for the left in Europe today, they must be looked for on the continent's western edge, in Dublin, Lisbon and, of course, Madrid.

Podemos has achieved a historic first in post-Franco Spain: a true coalition government. Many thought this scenario would never materialise. After the inconclusive April 2019 general election, the

PSOE (123 seats) and Podemos (42 seats) were unable to reach any sort of agreement. Prime Minister Pedro Sánchez refused to consider making Pablo Iglesias vice president and rejected Podemos's demands for ministerial posts. Iglesias very publicly said he was prepared to rule himself out of contention for the vice presidency, but refused to countenance any compact that didn't give the UP real power in the proposed government. With the menace of the far right increasing – the extreme-right Vox had entered Parliament with twenty-four seats – frustrated progressives demanded further concessions. But Iglesias stuck to his guns, arguing that entering government at any price was not the point of the party.

After months of gridlock and mutual recrimination, a tired and frustrated electorate went back to the polls in November. Vox doubled its representation to fifty-two seats, while Podemos's dropped to thirty-five. The new Parliament was strongly polarised, and the right was very close to regaining control of it. Progressive anger was quick to surface and targeted the PSOE for having precipitated another general election through its inability to negotiate a deal.

This time, with the further increased threat of the right looming, Sánchez moved quickly to form a government with Podemos, making Iglesias one of his vice presidents and integrating UP members into four ministerial posts: labour, equality, consumer affairs and universities. An emotional Iglesias was delighted by the turn of events, and declared that his biggest fear was letting his supporters down with an overly modest programme negotiated with the PSOE. Yet the victory, if one can call it that, was ironically as much a result of the electoral success of the right as of the left.

Despite being a marriage of convenience, the new coalition government rapidly moved forward with progressive policies (although differences over how best to address the fiscal implications of the coronavirus pandemic will test the parties' resolve to maintain a united front). Podemos is now in a stronger position to continue the valuable work it has been doing ever since it first entered Parliament in 2015. It brokered agreements with Sánchez's minority PSOE government in 2018 to raise the monthly minimum wage to 900 euros, introduce legislation for non-transferable maternity and paternity leave, and increase funding for public housing.

Today, as a participant in government, the party is swiftly building on those earlier initiatives. On 30 January 2020, the new coalition raised the monthly minimum wage to 950 euros. In the months since, several Podemos legislative initiatives have moved through Parliament, including the revocation of Article 52d (which allowed employers to dismiss people on medical leave), an increase to pensions in line with inflation and the declaration of a climate emergency. Vice President Iglesias and Ione Belarra, secretary of state for Agenda 2030 (the UN's sustainable development programme), have pushed for increased investment in social services, including healthcare and education, changes in housing legislation and the development of a national anti-poverty plan. Thanks to their efforts Spain has passed a historic minimum living income law to support the roughly 20 per cent of households living in severe poverty. The government has also moved quickly to pass legislation mitigating the drastic economic effects of the coronavirus pandemic, providing things such as rent support.

In one sense, the entry into government is a great success for Podemos – and for Iglesias, who kept his nerve in a difficult situation – but it is also a far cry from the hopes and dreams that propelled the party into existence in 2014. These opposing readings reflect the tensions inherent in hybrid 'movement parties' which maintain links to, and characteristics of, participatory social movements while at the same time trying to win state power through elections.

The British Labour Party, in contrast to Podemos, has always been an essentially parliamentary vehicle, but has also faced important tensions in recent years between MPs and an enlarged pro-Corbyn activist base. Understanding the internal dynamics of movement parties is important if we are to confront the challenges of contemporary democracy and increasing citizen dissatisfaction with 'actually existing democracy'.

Podemos was born in 2014 as a self-proclaimed citizens' initiative, and only later constituted itself as a political party – a process that has passed through two foundational congresses, Vistalegre I and II, with a third originally scheduled for the end of March 2020, but now postponed. It has always recognised its roots in the 15-M anti-austerity mobilisation that began in 2011. As Iglesias wrote in *New Left Review* in 2015: 'The principal social expression of the regime crisis was the 15-M movement. Its principal political expression has been Podemos.' Despite the many obstacles the party has faced (including spurious legal challenges, false allegations and fraudulent documents attempting to discredit it, none of which have held up in court), Podemos's gamble that it could channel widespread disaffection with established politics has paid off.

Spain's 15-M movement differed from previous waves of mobilisations in its 'democratic turn'. Prefigurative democracy, or horizontal autonomous organising, was no longer simply the structuring ideational framework through which other issues were confronted and developed – the modus operandi of movement groups addressing other issues, such as global justice, environmentalism, feminism and precarious labour. Instead, democracy became *the* central problematic into which all other issues were subsumed. Activists demanded *real* democracy, not just in their groups and subcultural milieux, but across the whole of society.

Podemos had to persuade activists to put their energies into an electoral initiative. This involved sustained strategic discursive work, and was initially very successful. The party integrated core elements of 15-M's political culture. While much of the early hype around Podemos concerned its digitally enabled democratic idealism, it is 15-M's feminist articulation of a politics of the commons – the result of sustained work by many feminist activists within the party and inspiration from feminist movements outside it – that has been its most significant contribution to the party. Ada Colau, mayor of Barcelona, and Manuela Carmena, former mayor of Madrid on the Podemos-supported coalition ticket, have been particularly influential in articulating this vision within and beyond the party.

Podemos – like Ada Colau, who also rose to power on the wave of the 15-M mobilisation, and in keeping with its self-identification as a hybrid party – has always insisted on the need for continued street mobilisation, through which citizens can make demands and apply pressure on the government, to help ensure that progressive parties actually pass progressive legislation. When Belarra took office as secretary of state for Agenda 2030, she opened the door to civil society organisations, arguing that Podemos needed a citizenry which 'demands ever more from us, because that is the only way we can move from words to acts and from promises to reality'.

But today, while Podemos is certainly the best party-political representative of 15-M's demands, it can only minimally be understood as a movement party. Such has been its internal transformation that some critics have characterised it as the least internally democratic party in Spain. Iglesias is the last man standing of the party's original founders, after a long process of internal defections or purges (depending on one's point of view, or who tells the story).

Following its breakthrough in the May 2014 European Parliament elections, the party had managed to bring on board a wide range of social movement actors, a remarkable achievement given the 15-M movement's initial aversion to representative politics. However, cracks started to appear at its first foundational congress that autumn. There were deep schisms over questions of party structure and decision-making processes, with some factions pushing strongly for greater internal democracy.

Paradoxically, participatory digital tools reinforced Iglesias's leadership at the expense of grassroots activists. The combination of a voting process open to everyone who wanted to register, and a hyper-mediatised environment where most party voters' only point of reference was likely to be what they saw of Iglesias on television, meant that those participants *less* involved in the party – not those who had taken part in preparatory circles and movement spaces ahead of the assembly – carried the day.

By Vistalegre II, differences between Iglesias and co-founder Íñigo Errejón had begun to surface, with Errejón's somewhat more horizontal or participatory proposals losing out once again to Iglesias's presidentialist approach. As Nuria Alabao put it, writing on the CTXT news site, 'The main tendencies within the party hoped for more decentralisation, more power for the grassroots and a more proportional system, but the bases have voted for more Pablo.'

Meanwhile, more and more people were leaving the party, and its electoral fortunes were declining. Podemos has lost votes and seats in every general election since the first one it contested in 2015 (it recorded a slight increase in seats in 2016, but this was an artefact of a joint party list). In 2018, Manuela Carmena, the popular mayor of Madrid who had been elected on a Podemos coalition platform known as Ahora Madrid, announced that she would be running for re-election the following year on an independent basis, taking with her several councillors who were promptly suspended from the party. Worse followed when Errejón, the most recognisable face in the party after Iglesias, and Podemos's presidential candidate for the Madrid regional elections, announced that he too would be running on Carmena's Más Madrid ticket.

Podemos faced a major image crisis. Iglesias immediately announced that Errejón had abandoned the party and moved quickly to replace him. Más Madrid won twenty seats in the regional election, Podemos only seven. In the municipal elections, meanwhile, Iglesias encouraged voters to support a rival candidate, Carlos Sánchez Mato, against Carmena. The latter won the popular vote, but lost the city hall to a right-wing coalition that included Vox. Sánchez Mato failed even to win the 5 per cent needed to obtain representation. Madrid had passed once again into the hands of the right, following the most progressive government it has ever had.

The repercussions of this catastrophe are still being felt, with each side blaming the other for the outcome. Errejón went on to create a new party, Más País, a few weeks before the November 2019 general election, attracting the support of former Podemos coalition parties Equo and Compromis, as well as members of various Podemos branches, further debilitating the party. While early polls predicted up to nineteen seats for Más País, in the event it won only three – still quite remarkable for a party formed such a short time before election day.

Although Unidas Podemos still has many excellent people

working within it, the loss of human capital over the past six years has been enormous. While some of the internal differences were probably too strong to be resolved, many other losses could have been avoided within a more democratic and pluralistic internal culture.

The latest loss is one of the party's most charismatic and popular figures, Podemos's Andalucían secretary general Teresa Rodríguez, of Anticapitalistas. Rodríguez announced that Anticapitalistas would not be attending Vistalegre III because Podemos had become a member of the political class it had been created to challenge, and Vistalegre III would be nothing more than the ratification of the subalternisation of Podemos to the PSOE.

Rodríguez and Iglesias disseminated a video in which they stand side by side and announce the departure of Adelante Andalucía from Podemos, due to differences of opinion over the formation of the PSOE coalition. At the end of the broadcast they embrace and reiterate that they will both continue to fight for the same things that led them to create Podemos in the first place. For me, the bittersweet moment is also tinged with a sense of appreciation for their explicit decision to use this small performative gesture – a hug – to model a different form of parting ways than the usual public recriminations.

As Podemos prepared for its third congress, Vistalegre III, no regional party group was planning to submit any proposals to the conference. There is no one left to challenge or even question Iglesias's leadership. But there is little left, either, of the promise offered by the original 'citizens' initiative' movement party. The contrast with the intense participation and debate of Vistalegre I – the widespread excitement and sense of possibility and hope – could not be more stark.

In a move that will accelerate Podemos's transformation from challenger movement to conventional party, Iglesias has introduced proposals to overturn three of the elements that differentiate it from the established parties: term limits, salary caps and free party membership. All three will be passed, as there is no longer any internal opposition or alternative current in the party. The first proposal extends term limits beyond the current twelve-year maximum, subject to consultation with party members (*inscritos*), clearing the way for Iglesias's continued leadership into the future. The second proposal delinks the cap on office-holder salaries from a ratio based on the minimum wage.

The third proposal pertains to party membership. In 2017 the party introduced a distinction between members and activists (*militantes*). Under the new proposal, and with the rationale that this will enable the party to maintain its financial independence from the banks, membership dues will be introduced for *militantes*. They alone will be able to participate and vote in the primaries for municipal-level posts. This will end the 'liquid' membership introduced in 2014 that allowed anyone aged fourteen or over to participate in party assemblies and circles. The sectoral 'circles' (nurses, teachers, etc.) will also disappear, leaving only territorial circles more similar to the regional associations of classical parties.

With these changes, some of the hallmarks of the party's hybrid identity are lost, and the transformation from a participatory grassroots to a presidentialist model is practically complete.

The term 'hybrid party' embraces an internal contradiction between movementist and party-political logics of collective action. Hybrid or movement parties need – initially at least – to maintain legitimacy in the eyes of their movement base. Podemos's initial success stemmed in large part from its ability to win

over grassroots support from Spain's progressive social movements, in the wake of 15-M. Whether it will be able to thrive as
a party in the absence of so many of its former supporters is an
open question. But never say never.

14

Hunger Gnaws at the Edges of the World

P. Sainath, Richard Pithouse and Vijay Prashad

What the International Monetary Fund calls the Great Lockdown sent 2.7 billion people, according to the International Labour Organization, into either full unemployment or near unemployment, with many one or two days away from desperate poverty and hunger. Starvation is already evident in many regions of the world. Social movements are doing what they can to organise horizontal forms of solidarity from below, but food riots are already a reality in India, South Africa, Honduras – everywhere, really. In many countries, states are responding with militarised force, with bullets rather than bread.

Before the pandemic, in 2014, the United Nations' Food and Agriculture Organization wrote: 'Current food production and distribution systems are failing to feed the world'. That is a damning statement. It needs to be taken seriously. Half-hearted measures are not going to work. We need a wide-reaching social revolution that breaks the grip of capital over the production and distribution of food.

Hunger is a bitter reality that modern civilisation should have expelled a century ago. What does it mean for human beings to learn how to build a car or fly a plane and not at the same time abolish the indignity of hunger? The old English reverend Thomas Malthus was wrong when he wrote that, for eternity, food production would grow arithmetically (1-2-3-4) and populations would grow geometrically (1-2-4-8), with the needs of the population easily outstripping the ability of humans to produce food. When Malthus wrote his treatise in 1789, there were about a billion people on the planet. There are now almost 8 billion people, and yet scientists tell us that more than enough food is produced to feed them all. Nonetheless, there is hunger. Why?

Hunger stalks the planet because so many people are dispossessed. If you do not have access to land, in the countryside or in the city, you cannot produce your own food. If you have land but no access to seed and fertiliser, your capacities as a farmer are constrained. If you have no land and do not have money to buy food, you starve. That's the root problem. It is simply not addressed by the bourgeois order, according to which money is god, land – rural and urban – is allocated through the market, and food is just another commodity from which capital seeks to profit. When modest food distribution programmes are implemented to stave off widespread famine, they often function as state subsidies for a food system captured, from the corporate farm to the supermarket, by capital.

Over the course of past decades, the production of food has been enveloped into a global supply chain. Farmers cannot simply take their produce to market; they must sell it into a system that processes, transports and then packages food for sale at a variety of retail outlets. Even this is not so simple, as the world of finance has enmeshed the farmer into speculation. In 2010, the United Nations' former special rapporteur on the right to food, Olivier De Schutter, wrote about the way that hedge funds, pension funds and investment banks overpower agriculture with speculation through commodity derivatives. These financial houses, he wrote, are 'generally unconcerned with agricultural market fundamentals'.* If there is any shock to the system, the entire chain collapses and farmers are often forced to burn or bury their food rather than allow it to be eaten. As Aime Williams writes of the situation in the United States, these are 'scenes out of the Great Depression: farmers destroying their products as Americans line up by the thousands outside food banks'.†

If you listen to agricultural workers, farmers and social movements around the world, you will find that they have lessons to teach us about how the system should be reorganised during this crisis. Here is a little bit of what we have learnt from them. It comprises a mix of emergency measures that can be implemented immediately and more long-term measures that can build towards sustained food security, and then food sovereignty – in other words, popular control over the food system.

- Enact emergency food distribution. Surplus stocks of food controlled by governments must be distributed to combat hunger. Governments must use their considerable resources to feed the people.

---

* Olivier De Schutter, 'Food Commodities Speculation and Food Price Crises', UN Special Rapporteur on the Right to Food, Briefing Note no. 2, September 2010.

† Aime Williams, 'US Restaurant Closings Spur Farmers to Destroy Food', *Financial Times*, 22 April 2020.

- Expropriate surpluses of food held by agribusiness, super-markets and speculators, and hand this over to the food distribution system.
- Feed the people. It is not enough to distribute groceries. Governments, alongside public action, must build chains of community kitchens where people can access real food.
- Demand government support for farmers who face challenges in harvesting their crops; governments must ensure that harvesting takes place following World Health Organization safety principles.
- Demand living wages for agricultural workers, farmers and others, regardless of whether they are able to work during the Great Lockdown. This must be sustained after the crisis. There is no sense in labelling workers as essential during an emergency and then disdaining their struggles for justice in a time of 'normality'.
- Provide financial support to encourage farmers to grow food crops, rather than turning to large-scale production of non-food cash crops. Millions of farmers in the poorer nations produce cash crops that richer nations cannot grow in their climate zones: it is tough to grow pepper or coffee in Sweden. The World Bank has 'advised' poorer nations to focus on cash crops to earn dollars, but this has not helped any of the small farmers who do not grow enough to support their families. These farmers, like their communities and the rest of human-ity, need food security.
- Reconsider the entanglement of the food supply chain, which involves the massive release of carbon into the atmosphere. Reconstruct food supply chains by region rather than along the lines of global distribution.

- Ban speculation of food markets by curbing derivatives and the futures exchange.
- Land – rural and urban – must be allocated outside the logic of the market, and systems must be established to ensure that food can be produced and the surplus distributed outside the control of corporate supermarkets. Communities should have direct control over local food systems.
- Build universal health systems, as called for by the Declaration of Alma-Ata in 1978. Strong public health systems are better equipped to constrain health emergencies. Such systems must have a strong rural component and must be open to all, including undocumented people.

The fact that so many people around the planet were going hungry before this crisis, including those living in the richest countries, is a profound indictment of the failures of capitalism. The fact that hunger is exploding exponentially during the crisis is a further indictment of capitalism. Hunger is among the most urgent of human needs, and immediate steps must be taken to get food to people in this crisis. But it is also vital that the social value of food – and with it, of land, rural and urban, and the means to produce food, such as seeds and fertiliser – is affirmed and defended against the socially ruinous logic of commodification and profit.

In 1943, the British Empire's bureaucrats took grain from Bengal and left the people in the grip of a terrible famine which killed between 1 million and 3 million people. Sukanta Bhattacharya, a member of the Communist Party of India who was nineteen at the time, edited a poetry anthology called *Akal* (Famine) for the Anti-Fascist Writers' and Artists' Association. In this

book, Bhattacharya published a poem called 'Hey Mahajibon'
(O Great Life!).

> O great life! No more of this poetry.
> Now bring the hard, harsh prose.
> Dissolve the tender poetic chimes.
> Strike the robust hammer of prose today.
>
> We do not need the tenderness of poetry.
> Poetry, today you can rest.
> A world devastated by hunger is prosaic.
> The full moon looks like burnt bread.

15

Building in All Directions

Jeremy Gilbert

Immediately prior to the introduction of pandemic emergency measures, the general state of left politics on either side of the Atlantic seemed clear. Bernie Sanders's second bid for the Democratic nomination appeared to be over, despite a heroic campaign, as the centrist establishment converged behind a revived Joe Biden candidacy. Jeremy Corbyn's leadership of the Labour Party – having culminated in a devastating electoral defeat in December 2019 – was about to end, leaving the left's preferred successor Rebecca Long-Bailey with no real hope of winning the contest against the more establishment-friendly Keir Starmer. Boris Johnson's government seemed secure and intent on carrying out its project of decisively breaking with Thatcher-ite neoliberal orthodoxy, aligning itself instead with the current wave of right-wing reaction against globalisation, cosmopolitan-ism and liberalism.

But although it would be easy to describe this simply as a moment of defeat for the left, this would be too simplistic and short-sighted an assessment. Both Corbyn's and Sanders's achievements must be understood against the backdrop of a historical phase, between 1988 and 2015, when the organised political left had been inactive as a political force in either country. Of course, there had been oppositional movements, labour organisations and left-wing publications, but the institutional left consisted almost entirely of residual elements, with little influence on wider public debate (outside universities) or mainstream politics. The scale of defeat suffered by the labour movement and the socialist left across the world during the 1980s had been so significant that many commentators had assumed that no recovery for it could ever be conceived, while any realistic assessment had to assume that, if possible at all, it would take decades.

Whether we see that recovery as beginning in the immediate aftermath of the 2008 financial crisis, in the various anti-austerity campaigns that sprang up around the world in 2011, or at any other time, it only became clearly visible and significant within mainstream electoral politics in 2015, when Corbyn became Labour leader and Sanders emerged as a credible contender for the 2016 nomination. It was always wildly optimistic to have expected the movements organised around these figures to rise from such a low base to the point of forming governments – governments that would have been the most radical for half a century – within the space of half a decade.

The fact that the recovery of the socialist left is not yet far enough advanced to be likely to gain state power in the US or the UK does not mean that it is unreal or insignificant. During the one-on-one debate with Sanders that apparently sealed Biden's bid for the candidacy, the most striking feature of the latter's discourse was the extent to which he appeared explicitly to accept – on behalf of the professional political class of which he has been such an assiduously loyal member – that, finally, the era of technocratic neoliberalism had drawn to a close. In the UK, while Corbyn's liberal centrist opponents remained stubbornly unwilling to accept this fact right through the disastrous election campaign, the Johnson government had clearly reached the same conclusion by the time of Rishi Sunak's first Budget.

The responses to the pandemic from both the Trump and the Johnson administrations have been astonishing in their scope. Both have shown their willingness to deploy many of the tools of the state in defence of universal minimum living standards. Of course, the moment of political uncertainty and conflict will come once the crisis is deemed to have passed, and capital begins to agitate for the long-term costs of those emergency measures to be transferred to workers and the public sector. And there is no question that, over the medium term, both quasi-fascist and ultra-technocratic responses to this crisis and to the impending climate catastrophe seem at least as likely to succeed as any kind of progressive governmental response. For now, however, it seems fair to suggest that, without significant socialist revival in recent years, these right-wing governments would not have moved so far or so fast to protect wages and living conditions.

So – the situation isn't all bad; but it clearly isn't all good either. For the revived left to have any hope of making further advances on this very difficult terrain, it is crucial to make a sober assessment of the current state of the forces ranged against it. In the UK, in the wake of the December 2019 election result, it is imperative to consider the long-term obstacles to any attempt to use the Labour Party as an exclusive vehicle for the advancement of socialist politics.

The fact is that the Labour Party has never – not once in its history – moved from opposition to winning a convincing parliamentary majority on a progressive platform. It has won elections when already in government or in wartime coalition, and it has won a tiny unworkable parliamentary majority from opposition. Tony Blair achieved a landslide victory in 1997 by promising Labour's traditional enemies in the media and the City of London that they would hold a veto over its programme in government. Since the 1980s, the Bennite tradition from which Corbyn came had comforted itself with the certainty that, if only it got the chance to lead the Party on a robust, explicitly socialist platform, it could sweep aside the forces of reaction and finally fulfil its destiny by winning a convincing parliamentary majority. Between 2017 and 2019, that theory was tested to destruction.

As I have argued several times elsewhere, the theory was always predicated on a catastrophic underestimation of the significance of two key institutional features of the British polity: the extraordinary bias of the established press (in England and Wales) towards an ideology of conservative English nationalism; and the fact that the 'first past the post' electoral system routinely advantages right-leaning populations of voters who tend to be more evenly spread across suburbs and rural areas, at the expense of those left-leaning constituents who tend to concentrate in cities. The only Labour leader within living memory to take full account of these factors was Blair; and his response was to tailor almost all of his policies and messaging to the prejudices of suburban swing voters and tabloid newspaper proprietors.

The question of what it would mean for the British left to take these factors seriously without simply abandoning any socialist project for Labour will remain absolutely crucial for the foreseeable future. But it is also critical to understand any attempt to address these specific problems in the context of the larger challenge to advance radical politics under relatively adverse conditions: the requirement to build winning coalitions.

Any political force that seeks to challenge established relations of power and inequality must build a broad coalition of social forces. This has been a political truism since at least the seventeenth century. Almost by definition, such a coalition must include sections of the population whose current orientation, self-conception and political consciousness diverge from those of the people who comprise the core of that force. While both the Corbyn and the Sanders movements had tremendous success in building support among forces aligned well to the left of their own explicit projects, each was defeated both by failing to attract enough middle-class liberal 'progressive' voters and by failing to convince enough working-class voters that the movement had the capacity to deliver its programme.

In the case of Labour's 2019 electoral defeat, far too much analysis has focused on one or other of these key factors rather than considering them together. In fact, for entirely understandable reasons, post-mortems have tended to result in contrary assertions about the political significance of the Brexit issue for Labour's losses between 2017 and 2019. From the 'hard' left of the Party, it has been frequently claimed that Labour's move away from a commitment to implement Brexit without a second referendum cost it crucial working-class votes and seats, dooming it to defeat. From other sections of the Party and the wider commentariat – including the 'soft' left – it has been repeatedly pointed out that Labour suffered catastrophic loss of votes (if not, to any great extent, of parliamentary seats) to the Liberal Democrats, Greens and Scottish National Party during the same period, largely because of strongly anti-Brexit voters deserting the Party. Still others have observed that many working-class voters ultimately seemed unconvinced that a Corbyn-led government could implement its socialist project, instead hoping that a Johnson-led Tory administration would at least offer them a measure of stability and modest economic improvement.

The truth is that all of these analyses are simultaneously true. At the same time, the fact is that Labour – including its pro-Brexit wing – never made any systematic effort to challenge the reactionary tabloid nationalism that clearly still plays a role in shaping the consciousness of many voters (especially older working-class voters outside metropolitan centres). The challenge for Labour and the wider left in the coming years will be to address not one or the other of these key obstacles to our project, but all of them simultaneously.

What would this look like in practice? On the one hand, there is no sane or rational approach to Labour's catastrophic electoral history that does not include an embrace of electoral reform, and cooperation with other parties committed to the same goals wherever possible. Much of the Corbynite left still reacts with revulsion to any suggestion of potential collaboration, in particular when it comes to the Liberal Democrats. Frankly, most of these responses seem based on a fundamental category mistake: they apply political and critical criteria that would be appropriate under pre-revolutionary conditions, when the commitment (or lack of it) to full socialism on the part of possible coalition partners would be a central issue of contemporary political debate. Clearly, we are not currently operating under such conditions, and neither are we likely to be any time soon.

The present historic context is such that the Corbynite left is neither large enough nor strong enough to challenge Conservative hegemony alone, while many other parties and organisations – from the Liberal Democrats to much of the NGO sector to the far left – experience the current pro-Tory bias of our media ecology and electoral system as highly debilitating factors which they all have a shared interest in overcoming. At the same time, the scale of the impending social crisis – both in the wake of a global pandemic and under accelerating climatic breakdown – is such that the need and opportunity to construct broad and inclusive coalitions have never been greater. This is not 1917. Our situation resembles, if anything, the emergency of 1939.

At the same time, there is no question that the greatest obstacle encountered by both the Corbynite left and the Sanders movement has been the limited capacity to organise poor workers, again outside metropolitan centres, and convince them of the viability of their programmes. In an essay such at this, it would be remiss to omit a clichéd remark calling for a determined effort to organise in workplaces and communities, to raise the consciousness and capacities of the working class, while challenging the propaganda of the right. This could have been said – and often has been said – at almost any point and in almost any place, since the earliest inception of the socialist movement. So what is most relevant to emphasise under present conditions is that this effort – crucial as it undoubtedly is – must take place in the context of a willingness to work with multiple organisations and to build a coalition that includes the more progressive sections of the liberal middle classes. Any exclusive emphasis on working-class organisation, on building the Labour Party or on strategic alliances with other parties and organisations will prove inadequate to our task. We must build our coalition out in all directions – to the left, to the right, into the sphere of mainstream media and deeper into the lives of our communities – if we are to have any chance of overcoming the obstacles that face us.

16

Global Capitalism Requires a Global Socialist Strategy

Ashok Kumar

In February 1972, Nixon went to China. While American bombers laid waste to the Vietnamese countryside with defoliants and explosive ordnance, killing and maiming inhabitants by the millions, Richard Nixon arrived in Beijing, where flashbulbs popped on the tarmac, and a giddy American press corps – already primed to call this 'the week that changed the world' – was ecstatic. An avowed anti-communist, Nixon – the first US president ever to visit the People's Republic – had crossed the Pacific to extend a historic offer. Officially, it was a gesture of peace. The US and China were not friends, but cordial acquaintances. A crisis in the global North necessitated a spatial solution to the global South.

With the global financial and monetary system of Bretton Woods deteriorating in the 1960s, US monetary imperialism underwent a major transformation. First, by suspending the gold convertibility of the dollar in 1971, US Federal Reserve Chair

Paul Volcker removed the cap on America's balance of payments. In an ingenious reversion, instead of acting as the world's creditor (drawing on its now-depleted gold reserves), the US would become its chief debtor. By greasing the wheels of commerce, and the palms of politics, with a flood of American treasury bonds, it would remain the world economy's 'indispensable nation', still capable of exercising outsized authority – but now through a more elastic financial instrument. The US reserved the right to threaten war should anyone try to call in the tab. But instead of underwriting reconstruction in Europe, it would use this liquidity to perfuse the late-industrialising nations – and in that regard, China, with its great reserves of labour, held the most potential.

Nixon's warm embrace had thawed party doctrine enough to allow for the rehabilitation of figures such as Deng Xiaoping, a party elder whose pragmatic approach to economics – striving to harness capitalism – had seen him relegated to anonymous factory work. In the coming years, Deng would, after some jockeying, succeed Mao Zedong as a paramount leader and proceed to institute sweeping reforms, opening China up to flows of international learning, technology and – most importantly – capital. The ensuing boom in manufacturing saw China become the new 'workshop of the world', replacing the US. Meanwhile, America – the single biggest market for Chinese goods – would undergo a complementary transition, as its own capital-light industries gave way to services and leveraged consumption.*

The most salient of Deng's reforms was the creation of special economic zones, or SEZs, first in the south-east of the country, in

---

* This arrangement tends to lock in austerity/underconsumption for Chinese workers, since it is based on the precondition of low-wage, labour-intensive industry. However, beyond low-wage/high-wage dichotomies, there is also a pattern in the neoliberal global order of 'producer-savers' (that is, Germany and China) and 'consumer-debtors' (the US).

Guangdong and Fujian provinces, and then dotted up the coast and inland, as Beijing conferred the new status on several major ports and provincial capitals. This experimental designation – the brainchild of Xi Zhongxun, father of Xi Jinping and the then governor of Guangdong – allowed for relaxed regulatory regimes and the lifting of tariffs, with the aim of stimulating, but not revolutionising, the economy. Originally conceived as a quick way to stem the outflow of Guangdong Chinese into neighbouring Hong Kong, where wages and living standards were much higher, SEZs supercharged the local economy. Soon, the designation became a means of creating boom towns by fiat.

The first SEZ, Shenzhen, had been a sleepy fishing village just north of Hong Kong, with a population of about 30,000 in 1979 – the size of Beloit, Wisconsin. By 2018, only forty years later, it had grown into an administrative area with over 20 million residents – the size of metropolitan New York City. Beijing accommodated the vast sums of FDI (foreign direct investment) pouring into China by encouraging internal migration to the SEZs and channelling new tax revenues into infrastructure (especially transport networks) to keep down capital costs. This willingness to invest in infrastructure while suspending labour, trade and environmental regulation dovetailed nicely with China's natural advantages in raw materials and workforce size and nourished a manufacturing revolution, which transformed the country into an export powerhouse.

This process – the fall of the so-called Bamboo Curtain – is usually described in triumphalist terms by free marketeers who laud the successful 'integration' of China into the world economy and the emergence of a domestic bourgeoisie. But such talk obscures the devil's bargain at the heart of it all, since it is

the Chinese Communist Party (CCP) that steered this course
and remains at the helm. Under Mao and his central planning
regime, which used lessons gleaned from early Soviet history,
the economy had been designed to achieve wage parity and maximum employment, preventing the emergence of a real market
for labour.

But under Deng, the 'iron rice bowl' (public sector jobs guar-
anteeing steady pay and benefits) began to shrink as structural
unemployment and worker competition were gradually rein-
troduced. In due time, it seemed that the CCP was organising
workers solely for the sake of capital – that is, to produce the
labour market conditions necessary to attract more FDI. In terms
of GDP, this new tactic was a wild success: the economy grew at
some 10 per cent per annum – the fastest pace in recorded history.
By the late 2000s, Chinese GDP had surpassed Japan's and China
had become the world's second-largest economy.

The majority of early FDI, however, came not from the West,
but from the Han diaspora in Taiwan, Hong Kong, Macau and
Singapore, whose special privileges allowed its members – and
select firms in Malaysia and South Korea – to form what became
known as 'dragon multinationals'. These firms grew rapidly and
became gravity wells for outsourced production, especially in the
most labour-intensive sectors. Bulk purchasing orders flooded in
from Western clothing brands.

The mass shift in global production towards China and other
emerging economies transformed distribution and consumption
by creating GVCs (global value chains), allowing transnational firms to capture substantially larger surpluses. These new
profits were derived from the difference in 'markup' caused by
'global labour arbitrage', or international unequal exchange
relation. And so, as unit labour costs in China dropped, the cost

advantages of production there grew. It was the economic crisis in the advanced capitalist world that allowed ostensibly political conflicts to be put aside.

Monopoly and monopsony in the GVC

A firm is said to have a monopoly when it is the sole seller of a good in a market. Similarly, an oligopoly is a market dominated by a limited number of sellers. A monopsony, however, is the inverse of a monopoly, meaning a market with a single buyer. And, oligopsony, by extension, is the inverse of an oligopoly, meaning a market with only a limited number of buyers. Therefore, the degree of monopoly is the relative degree of oligopoly in a market and the degree of monopsony is the relative degree of oligopsony in the value chain. Oligopoly and oligopsony both describe markets with imperfect competition, that is, a stark asymmetry in the balance between buyers and sellers. It follows from this that the degree of monopoly (the ratio of sellers to buyers) in a market is the inverse of the degree of monopsony (the ratio of buyers to sellers).

A higher degree of monopsony power (DMP) necessarily leads to a higher share in value obtained by global buyers (well-known brands and retailers). The spatial specificities of production, combined with changes in the distribution of value, lead to consolidation and change in DMP. When the balance of competitive forces resolves temporarily into a symbiotic state, the spatial fixes used by buyers (capital flight) are exhausted, thus lowering DMP. This change, in turn, provides suppliers with more bargaining power. Capitalistic competition, therefore, produces oligopolies at either end of the supply chain, leading to crises of profitability and attempts at new 'fixes'. In the 1970s, the fix was spatial (globalisation); today, it arrives through the organisational and/ or technological route.

This argument can be traced back to Adam Smith, who posited an inverse relationship between profit and capital stock caused by intensified competition and consequent innovation. Rudolf Hilferding also argued that in certain specific historical conditions, competition could hinder long-term accumulation. The claim here is therefore twofold. First, labour-intensive sectors (such as garments, footwear, toys, furniture, etc.) that employ much of the global industrial working class are defined by the logic of competition, which moves them inexorably in the direction of consolidation, thereby reducing the monopsonistic power of buyers. Second, changes in the value chain are reflected in the bargaining power of workers.

The working conditions in the most labour-intensive industries cannot be understood without reference to the composition of capital at the level of the value chain. These value chains (namely footwear and garments) remain vertically disintegrated, buyer-driven and technologically underdeveloped. The emergence of value chains in these sectors has intensified a global 'race to the bottom', magnifying the asymmetry of power between suppliers and buyers through the maintenance of a high degree of control by global 'buyers'.

Globalised brands exercise monopsony power over producers through their ability to select from a large pool of outside firms for almost every phase of the value chain – textiles, production, transport, processing, warehousing, and so on. Suppliers unable to reach the price demanded by these transnational brands risk the loss of orders or even closure. This dependence has left manufacturers in a state of perpetual instability, unable to muster the capital necessary to escape the orbit of brand power and pursue their own development, and with the possibility of losing a purchasing contract an inexorable existential threat. The result is that workers in these sectors have the lowest bargaining power of any industrial sector.

The immediate consequence of the COVID-19 pandemic was falling demand and growing instability in the supply chain. The result was the bankruptcy of smaller suppliers whose margins were thin even at the best of times. Larger suppliers increased their market share at the expense of these smaller firms, expanding horizontally and vertically, and helping to initiate the process of investment in technology, which increased barriers to entry to new firms. This reduced the degree of monopsony in the global value chain.

Take the garment sector in Bangladesh, which is an industrial one-trick pony. Eighty-four per cent of its export revenue comprises readymade garments which workers, mostly women, churn out chiefly for Western markets. However, since the COVID-19 pandemic, global demand has plummeted, brands and retailers have cut and run and factories have shut down, laying off a million garment workers – a quarter of the country's garment workforce.

On 27 May, the Bangladesh Garment Manufacturers and Exporters Association (BGMEA), the country's largest trade group for garment factory owners, wrote to British billionaire Philip Day's Edinburgh Woollen Mill (EWM), which owns brands such as Jaegar and Peacocks, demanding that the group pay for clothes shipped prior to 25 March and threatening to blacklist the company. BGMEA president Rubana Huq suggested that targeting EWM was only the beginning. The move was unprecedented in the history of the sector and reveals larger processes of change in global industrial capitalism.

Workers and socialist strategy

Employment relations can in part be explained by the conflicts between capital and labour. Labour is, after all, the only living and subjective factor in production. In Marxian terms, labour is an employer's 'variable capital' – variable in that it is elastic: the degree of exploitation involved (and, therefore, profitability) can be increased by cutting pay, extending the workday or intensifying the workday.

As outlined above, deregulation led to a higher degree of monopsony (high ratio of suppliers to buyers). Thus, as competition increased at the bottom of the supply chain, factory owners were under constant pressure to produce more for less. Those who could somehow keep pace would be rewarded with big contracts. Those who could not would go under. As trade barriers to Latin America, South and South-East Asia and most importantly China withered away, transnational competition intensified, turning local regulations into hindrances and productivity into a religion. In these circumstances, where other variables were effectively controlled by the absence of capital reserves at the point of production, a factory's survival came down to what could be wrung from workers at the least expense.

Just as deregulation intensified competition at the bottom of the supply chain, it also brought down the price a buyer was willing to pay a supplier for the production of a commodity. Over time, fewer firms were able to produce that product for the price demanded by buyers, which winnowed the number of suppliers in the supply chain. The resulting falling monopsony power increased the value captured by these now more consolidated firms. Consolidation increases the surviving suppliers' share of value, which expands access to finance, facilitates self-investment and raises entry barriers.

Labourers employed in the 'key nodes' of globally integrated production systems possess greater bargaining power (workplace bargaining power) vis-à-vis capital, which can affect the entire value chain and production network. However, subcontracting and 'vertical disintegration' were introduced to erode that power. Spatially and organisationally flexible production systems are therefore a tool for controlling labour costs by constraining labour's power. And while the cynical but savvy exploitation of uneven development led to a system of world production centred on the global North, it appears that the next stage of development is already on the horizon. The year 2010 was the first in which the economies of the global South accounted for half of all FDI inflows. This, coupled with the year-on-year increase in FDI outflows from those same economies – the 2011 UNCTAD report notes that 'emerging economies are the new FDI power-houses', and that most outflows stayed within the global South – indicates their growing significance as sites of production and consumption, and as sources of investment.

Industrial workers have low bargaining power where surpluses are limited, and production is diffuse and isolated from consumption. Deregulation and increased competition, however, have created more centralised industries within historically labour-intensive sectors. Oligopolistic power translates into higher profits, which are being stretched with finance and invested in labour-saving technologies. However, when buyer DMP falls, suppliers ascend, giving workers the high ground. Indeed, with the onset of the coronavirus crisis, we are witnessing the consequences of years of overreach by brands and of the growth, consolidation and organisation of suppliers in the apparel industry. We now see fewer and fewer suppliers dominating specific sectors of production.

In the 1970s, capital globalised in order to confront its crisis of profitability. It sought new terrains of profitability in China, Bangladesh and across the global South. Today, capital seeks a new means to fix its now global crisis. The strategy of stageism, of accelerating the conditions of capitalism to arrive at socialism, died in 1953. It's clear that socialism will not arrive from above, but must be built from below. The COVID-19 pandemic is making visible many of capitalism's abstractions. The new conditions of increasingly fortified states, national chauvinism and the uneven distribution of global capitalism require an extra-parliamentary and extra-national strategy. This strategy necessitates a predictive analysis of a highly integrated global production process, including mapping the logics that shape its contours, identifying its key chokepoints and nodes, and building links between workers and their organisations to maximise their disruptive power.

17

Making It Count: Resisting the Authority of Ignorance

Sita Balani

[It's] utterly absurd and wrong that you can read out on air a tweet coming in from one of your readers which calls the prime minister a liar. I think it is amazing you can do that.

Stanley Johnson

Just as no misconduct on the part of a father can free his children from obedience to the fifth commandment (to honour one's father and mother), so no misgovernment on the part of a King can release his subjects from their allegiance.

James I, *Basilikon Doron*

There is an anti-elitist piety, often expressed by the academic or media branch of the same broad elite, that refuses to accept the specialness of rulers.

David Goodhart

Living in the UK in the time of COVID-19 means living in a world in which representation exercises brutal dominion over reality. If propaganda is usually laced into the fabric of everyday life, woven through its textures, sewn into speech, now it feels like a heavy cloth laid over reality as we stumble in the dark beneath. Claustrophobic, we sleep too much or we don't sleep at all; words of prayer, long dormant, form on our lips; we wait and wait for the bread to prove and then forget to bake it; our dreams, achingly vivid, full of water and touch and terror, linger in the late morning sun.

Even for many with the resources to (self-)isolate, death shadows the edges of our vision. Though there has been much talk of the psychological impact of the *lockdown*, we've seen little discussion of the psychological effect of the *death toll*. Watching the daily count grow (103 ... 209 ... 563 ... 1,019 ...) and knowing that it could have been otherwise weighs heavy, slicker than shame, more potent than guilt. The time lag between infection and sickness, between sickness and hospitalisation, between hospitalisation and death, produces a novel form of dread, an embodied and insuppressible knowledge. We are quickly learning, however, that knowledge alone is not power.

Knowing that people are going to die unless something is done to prevent their deaths is not the same as being able to stop it. The psychological effects of being governed by pathological liars, buffoons and brutish aristocrats might be just as significant as those produced by enforced isolation. That their governance, in its callousness and arrogance, appears to be accepted by the majority adds a sticky layer to the dread. What will it take to tear the cloth? What will it take to make the truth count? We can read papers on epidemiology, we can make spreadsheets and graphs, but we cannot make the evidence *matter*. That we are free to speak does not mean we can communicate. The emotional impact of the days spent shouting and screaming and ranting, cajoling and begging and reasoning, and of the days spent consuming and producing meticulous evidence online, all to no effect, may be as debilitating as our loneliness.

As governments around the world announced lockdowns, as borders began to shut, as the death toll rose in Europe, the UK government continued to make light of the virus: it was just the flu, wash your hands, take it on the chin. When a lockdown was finally announced – looser than elsewhere, with less financial support, and plenty of loopholes exploitable by unscrupulous employers – it was too little, too late. With no sign of an effective system to suppress or control infection rates, we wondered whether this disaster was the result of incompetence or malice. Were they trying to kill us or simply happy to watch us die? In the end, hubris has emerged as the more viable answer: it is the myth of British exceptionalism that fertilises the soil from which both malice and incompetence grow.

Positing the idea that Britain is uniquely stupid could lend itself to an inverted nationalism, a turning of the pyramid that leaves its basic structures intact. After all, the authoritarian obsession with instinct over analysis, feeling over fact, has turned the loose sediment of anti-intellectualism into a cornerstone of the Brexit project. Boris Johnson's marked refusal to fall into line behind the rest of Europe, as well as much of the rest of the world, is highly revealing. Britain's nineteenth-century victory in the 'game' of competitive colonialism has deformed the national political culture along the lines of a particular delusion of grandeur, as well as a longstanding belief that politics is mere sport. The US's similar handling of the crisis suggests that imperialism deforms the political capacities of its supposed victors as well as destroying the lives of its victims.

The lurid spectacle of Donald Trump's press conferences – in which he berates journalists and advises the American people to inject bleach into their veins – has rightly been the subject of global condemnation. But the difference between Trump's surreal, late-night-shopping-channel sleaze and Johnson's bluster is not one of degree but of style. When Johnson fears the bluster won't work, he simply disappears. The daily press conferences are given by any number of Tory ministers, many relatively unknown until recently, and various public health officials and scientific advisors, whose lies are more shocking than those told by the politicians. Across the board, these briefings are an exercise in dissimulation executed with all the cunning of a spoilt child. They know we know they are lying. But with no mechanism to hold them to account, the lies simply don't matter.

The media could make this spectacle a daily reckoning, but in the absence of any actual desire to seek the truth, their presence simply offers a simulacrum of democratic process. When a journalist ventures a more committed line of questioning – for example, why do we have the highest death rate in Europe? – the government's response is not only evasive but wounded. The ministers are doing their best. If Joe Public can't keep himself alive, why should *they* be held responsible?

This open contempt for the public is not new – it was there when Jacob Rees-Mogg claimed that those who lost their lives in the Grenfell fire lacked common sense; it was there when Prime Minister Johnson hid in a fridge to avoid public scrutiny; it was there when Stanley Johnson, his father, referred to the public as illiterate. But it is at its most insidious when even hypocrisy, the accountability of the weak, no longer has any traction. It should have come as no surprise to see the government assert that the chosen few, including Dominic Cummings, are above the law. Conservatism of all stripes is, in the end, a defence of inequality. While neoliberalism rationalised inequality through meritocracy – thereby more easily sustaining the rhetoric of liberal democracy – Johnsonism is a bolder, more capricious assertion of social hierarchy: in place of aspiration, private property and individual success, it offers merely a bullish defence of entitlement.

Primarily concerned with Johnson's own almost monarchical sense of entitlement to govern, the white entitlement of England's beleaguered natives supplies the justificatory rationale. Of course, the most profound and effective mechanism we have devised to defend social hierarchy is racism. Though racism might begin by differentiation – by valuing some lives at the expense of others – it opens the door for the devaluation of all human life at the hands of the powerful. In the coronavirus crisis, we can see that the explicit assertion of ruling-class impunity is made possible by the longstanding disregard for the lives of black and brown people.

Despite this grim situation, many on the left have been quick to conjure a utopian future. Think pieces about the post-pandemic world proliferate – a Green New Deal, the resurgence of the unions, a four-day week, a new social contract, an end to the family – as though revolutionary change is inevitable. We need to imagine a better future, of course, but the rapid reach for box-fresh solutions is its own kind of hubris. As Les Back notes, 'Hopeful possibility and action can be sustained without necessarily being hostage to the belief that everything is going to improve.'

The rush towards a false dawn is a symptom of our inability to live with the pandemic, to live within its warped temporality.

Arundhati Roy's concept of the pandemic as portal has been taken up, but it may be a matter of years, not months, before we reach the other side. In her original piece, the metaphor of the portal is one that carries as much foreboding as it does hope: we may well drag the 'carcasses of our prejudice' along on our backs; they may be given new and destructive life in the process. There are no guarantees. What at first appeared to be a holding space between one world and the next may be a much longer interregnum; it may not be an interregnum at all. We must attend to the politics of the portal; we must learn to be present here, now.

While there is little cause for optimism, there may be reason to hope. As the crisis began to bite, local support networks sprang up like mushrooms. The initial groups – started by anarchists borrowing from Pyotr Kropotkin's conception of mutual aid – did not need the British public to commit to anarchism in order to thrive. Within hours, there were tens of thousands of people joining WhatsApp groups with their neighbours; within days, there were close to a million. Despite the inconsistent political character of these groups (with a Neighbourhood Watch tendency rivalling the initial left-wing impulse), this level of spontaneous organisation perturbed members of government, who increasingly see the public as a kind of market competitor, as well as an unruly object, in the business of social control. The government quickly set up its own (predictably) app-based alternative – NHS Volunteer Responders – to suture some of the gaping wounds created by austerity and to undermine the mutual aid network. Over 750,000 signed up, but a month later, only 75,000 tasks had been logged. The organisation was essentially a website, a digital sign-up sheet for nothing. The mutual aid network, on the other hand, continues to bed in, growing deeper roots, creating new pathways for sociality, hyper-localised yet everywhere.

The use of NHS branding for Johnson's phantom army of volunteers is worth pausing at. The refrain that we must act to 'protect the NHS' has been a clear attempt to capitalise on, and control, the collective loyalty to our nationalised healthcare. But to protect the NHS rather than the health of the people cleaves the health service from its purpose. Boris Johnson can applaud cuts to the health service, and then applaud the health service itself, because those three magical letters have become a fetish object. That the NHS was not, during this first wave of the virus, 'overwhelmed' is the result of an unspoken, unacknowledged system of triage, which left people to die at home or on the regular ward down the hall from the ICU. But healthcare workers, despite strict orders to keep silent, continue to speak out about the lack of PPE, the staffing shortages, the ghost wards of the Nightingale hospitals. Every healthcare worker who refuses to endorse the 'Clap for Carers' is roundly attacked on social media, but their insistence pierces the façade.

The displacement of reality by bunting and nationalist bluster, by shiny blue apps and astroturfed VE Day street parties, depends on ignorance. It is telling that David Goodhart's defence of the 'specialness' of rulers proclaimed that 'the combination of mass higher education and social media threatens to make society ungovernable'. Goodhart may be misguided here about the revolutionary power of social media, but the civil servant who tweeted 'can you imagine having to work with these truth twisters?' demonstrated some unexpected possibilities.

Goodhart may also be mistaken as to the power of higher education in its current, commodified form, but he inadvertently exposes the ways in which authoritarianism depends on ignorance. Ignorance here is no accident, no mere absence of knowledge, but a quality ruthlessly, shamelessly cultivated. We might think of ignorance as an authoritarian epistemology – one dismissive of tested knowledge, one that shrugs off openness and debate, that treats all challenge or critique as treason. Ignorance is the product of the elites presented as the authentic sensibility of the working class. Ignorance is powerful, but not omnipotent. We ought to take up Goodhart's challenge. We must make ourselves ungovernable, by whatever means necessary.

We have been in training to live in their world. They have been training us. But we have also been teaching each other how to live against their world – how to live in defiance of it, to outsmart it, outrun it, out-love it. We must find a way to cultivate these counter-pedagogies, to reach beyond the logic of the moment. When workers refuse to dance to the tune of nationalism, and insist on a reality beyond the authoritarian spectacle, we see the possibility of turning the government's discourse inside out, exposing the rot. When we contribute to the funeral costs of a stranger, we tell someone, somewhere, that they do not face their loss alone. In the voices of the dead, the dying, the grieved, in the actions of the carers and the cared for, we can find a kind of hope – not an optimism, but the commitment to truth needed to force a confrontation with reality.

18

Finance and Left Strategy

James Meadway

This chapter is being written in the early stages of what is likely to become the biggest financial crisis in human history. The COVID-19 pandemic is disrupting the most fundamental economic institution – the labour market – and from this disruption, all other crises follow: the collapse of demand and extraordinary decline in GDP; the rolling crises of bankruptcies and failed investment; and of course a global financial crisis. Unlike the crisis of 2008–9, sometimes used as a benchmark, this is one that begins in the 'real' economy, before spreading to the financial realm.

This inversion should shift the focus of attention. COVID-19 requires the immediate winding back of much economic activity, alongside the provision of protections to allow people to cease their activities safely, while organising essential services such as food supply, healthcare and broadband. This is not so much a wartime economy as an *anti*-wartime economy: a grand demobilisation in the interests of public health. COVID-19 will be a transformational event in global economic history: it is a crisis *sui generis*; there is simply no comparable moment in the history of capitalism. But it is possible to discern, already, some of its impacts: an acceleration of 'deglobalisation', as finance, trade and perhaps travel retrench behind national borders; the continued expansion of the state in economic life; and the expansion and reinforcement of the data economy in all aspects of our lives.

As Grace Blakeley has recently highlighted in *Stolen* (2019), but as radicals have warned since the late nineteenth century, the position of the financial system in Britain creates a specific set of strategic, long-term problems for any project seeking to make the country even a little fairer. At least since the end of the 1970s, the problem of how to manage a globalising financial system has occupied the left's strategic horizons: on two occasions in Europe, great hopes were raised by would-be reforming governments – François Mitterrand's presidency in France in 1981, and Syriza in Greece in 2015 – only to be seemingly dashed by the machinations of international finance.

This reading of events is, in fact, a little confused: in both cases, political considerations relating to the demands of European integration did far more damage. For Mitterrand, reneging on domestic reflation (increased public spending, nationalisation, wage increases) was the price to pay for retaining a strong franc and charting a course towards a single currency; for Greece, the far tighter bind was euro membership and the European Central Bank's effective control over the monetary system. It is hard to attribute either to 'global finance'. Domestic considerations mattered more, even if these were directed towards international goals.

The critical issue for the left, at least in larger developed economies, has always been the requirement to deal with the domestic impact of finance and the international *political* relationships it imposes, rather than 'financial markets' as such. For New Labour, a 'light touch' approach to financial regulation allowed its leaders to ignore these challenges. While the credit still flowed, this seemed to work, and New Labour in office became a reliable cheerleader for Britain's financial services industry. Once that flow of credit had dried up, as the monstrous credit bubble of the 1990s and the 2000s burst in the great financial crisis, the entire New Labour project was sunk. The financial system reached a globalised high in 2007: cross-border financial flows are down nearly 65 per cent on that year's peak volume, probably never to return. By failing to address issues of *domestic* political economy within a large and internationalised financial system, New Labour worsened the impact of a global crisis over which it fundamentally had no control.

But the crash revealed two further unpleasant facts about Britain's financial system. The first is one common to all countries where the financial sector has become large relative to the rest of the economy. When finance becomes too big and powerful, it tends to distort economic decision making. In conventional economic parlance, it leads to a 'misallocation of capital', as credit gets steered away from longer-term investments in, for example, growing businesses, in favour of short-term easy returns into assets such as London property.*

The second became apparent only in the teeth of the 2008–9 crisis: the dependency of a very large and internationalised financial system on the ready supply of dollars. When these dollars dried up, the Federal Reserve – acting, in effect, as a global lender

---

* Resource misallocation is estimated by the International Monetary Fund to have been substantially worse in the UK, post-crash, than in other European countries. See Anna Bordon, Mico Mrkaic and Kazuko Shirono, 'United Kingdom: Selected Issues', IMF Country Report 16/58, February 2016, p. 22.

of last resort – opened 'swap lines' to the major central banks of the world, granting them fast, reliable access to cheap dollars that could be supplied to their own banking systems.* By allowing the UK's financial system to grow unfettered, and extend itself across the globe, New Labour created a major *political* dependency on decisions taken in the US. Without the swap lines, the UK banking system would have collapsed.

A distorted British economy and a deepening dependency on the US were the *domestic* consequences of the ballooning financial system. These two problems have political solutions: in both cases, the requirement is both to shrink the size of finance relative to wider economic activity, and to restructure it, breaking up large institutions and creating an ecosystem of different financial institutions.

The 2017 Manifesto contained some proposals for the transformation of the financial system: breaking up the mostly public-owned Royal Bank of Scotland; promoting a wider ecology of smaller financial institutions; and expanding state financing itself, in the form of a £250 billion National Investment Bank and the essential regional development banks. It did not amount to a comprehensive programme for finance, but it set a clear direction of travel. The manifesto identified that it was necessary to think about how to reshape the private sector banking system, and that establishing a diversity of institutions was an essential part of this.

Between 2017 and the 2019 Manifesto, two outstanding background papers were produced – 'A New Public Banking Ecosystem' and 'Finance and Climate Change' – by independent researchers commissioned by the Shadow Treasury team. But

---

* Adam Tooze's *Crashed* (London, 2018) provides the best single account of this episode.

the first concentrates only on creating a *public* banking system, and the second proposes technical modifications to the existing banking and finance regulations. The wider strategic imperative raised in the 2017 Manifesto – of a structural change encompassing the *whole* of banking – had been dropped. The major changes were to be made solely on the public sector side, through institution building.

In this sense, the 2019 Manifesto – expansive as it was – was significantly *less* radical than the manifesto of just two years before. It was utopian, in the double sense that it proposed an alternative world but also offered few ideas on how it could be achieved. But relative to this dual-use utopianism, the manifesto's actual ambitions were modest. The scheme to decarbonise the economy, for example, was impressive in its policy detail, but sorely lacking in its political strategy, above all on the question of prioritisation: how was the civil service to do all this while ending austerity, repairing the NHS and building council homes to the value of £70 billion?

The de-prioritisation of finance reflects the nature of the political period: the further we move from the great financial crisis of 2008–9, the less pressing the issue seems to be; and the sector has gone through a genuine, and important, shift in the intervening years. Campaigning front and centre on the issue of finance would have been a peculiar choice in 2019. But its absence weakened the manifesto, reflecting a weakness that developed in Corbynism over the period from 2017 to 2019: the substitution of government action and bureaucratic fixes for a political strategy aimed not only at winning an election, but at implementing meaningful changes once there.

The latter issue is not simply a managerial problem – a question of ensuring that plans handed to the civil service are prioritised and followed through. Rather, it is a question of what action can be taken before entering government, such as building alliances, creating a broad social consensus around the changes needed and immediately implementing changes on the ground where possible – whether by local authorities, including moves to set up local authority banks, or in wider civil society. In short, effective strategy involves working towards a genuinely hegemonic conception of how social change might be won in conditions where the left's traditional bases of social support are weakened.

There is an unresolved tension here between what we could think of as centralising or decentralising tendencies – or, perhaps, 'socialism from above' versus 'socialism from below'. What we might call a Keynesian economic strategy – making the state bigger, with the post-war consensus as a reference point – became, over time, the dominant element in Labour's economic programme, to the detriment of the more politically fruitful decentralising elements.

As Boris Johnson's programme – even before COVID-19 – has demonstrated, Keynesian interventions, up to and including the suppression of finance, can lead us further and deeper into an authoritarian future. There is no necessary contradiction between combining stricter controls on trade unions and the deregulation of labour markets on the one hand, with raising government investment and pushing industrial policy on the other. The intellectual error would be to maintain that the expansion of the state *necessarily* represents a positive alternative to capitalism as such and that the suppression of finance *necessarily* represents a progressive moment.

With state functions so whittled away that, at the time of writing, public health services stand on the brink of coronavirus-induced collapse, the desire to demand that government undertake the necessary action to secure the continued functioning of civil society is understandable. But these demands represent the bare minimum; and they come at a price. The price of a decidedly Keynesian intervention imposed by Conservative chancellors in the immediate wake of the financial crisis was a decade of the worst austerity this country has known for generations – and, via the overhaul of the regulatory regime, the securing of the financial system's pre-eminent position inside the British economy. States and banks across the developed world became intertwined in the post-crash period, forming a 'sovereign-bank nexus'.* Often, the tools of financial repression most beloved of reformers – macroprudential regulation, for example – have simply served to stabilise and preserve the status quo. Deliberate government action – for instance in cutting the bank levy to favour a separate profits tax – similarly shifted the balance of power in favour of the larger banks, while effective sector lobbying helped defang even the fairly mild recommendations proposed by the Vickers commission.

The point here is not merely that finance is a powerful lobby that continues to shape government policy; it is that the post-crash balance between state and finance was one not of simple opposition, but of mutual *reinforcement*. Further regulation has not resulted in the diminution of the power of finance, but something like its preservation in aspic. It has taken two events to shift that: Brexit, and now – on a vastly greater scale – COVID-19.

We do not know what price the Conservative government will place on the current round of Keynesian interventions it is undertaking. It is possible that a period of accelerated austerity will be imposed, with the *Economist* among those already arguing for a

---

* Giovanni Dell'Ariccia, Caio Ferreira, Nigel Jenkinson et al., 'Managing the Sovereign-Bank Nexus', ECB Working Paper Series no. 2177, September 2018.

winding back of the state once the immediate crisis has passed. The French government has proposed abolishing various labour protections. By far the most significant longer-term outcome, however, will be the deepening and extension of the data economy. The need for testing and monitoring as part of a suppression strategy to contain the virus has already led to the appearance of more intrusive data collection methods in China and South Korea. Early on in the crisis, Dominic Cummings hosted a Number 10 meeting with leading data companies, including Facebook, Google and Peter Thiel's security-focused private enterprise, Palantir.

There will be distinct challenges to finance from a post-COVID-19 world: the elevated costs of environmental risk, including further epidemics and pandemics (what the Bank of International Settlements labelled 'green swans'), but also the potential challenge posed to Big Tech incumbents' business models by their desire to move into financial services. Slowly emerging in front of us is a combination of state, finance and data that could easily accelerate a decline into authoritarianism. A Keynesian response to this, which sought simply to expand the size of the state further, would be obviously inadequate. The left must return to its decentralising and democratic roots, promoting wider forms of common ownership across the economy, including in the finance sector.

19
Green Socialism
Chris Saltmarsh

In the period between the economic crises of 2008 and 2020, socialism and environmentalism converged within growing democratic socialist movements on either side of the Atlantic. The rise of Bernie Sanders and Jeremy Corbyn appeared to offer shortcuts to state power for socialists and climate activists who had made limited progress in previous years. Could two of the nation states most culpable for the ecological crisis really have their liberal democracies captured by democratic socialists simultaneously?

Labour went into the December 2019 general election with the most ambitious climate justice policies of any party in Europe, largely as a result of activism by the campaign Labour for a Green New Deal, which successfully pushed the Party towards a radical environmentalist platform commensurate with the scale of the climate crisis.

The Labour for a Green New Deal campaign aimed to take advantage of the political space opened up by Corbyn's leadership. Its co-founders had backgrounds in grassroots climate organising, student movements, internationalist solidarity and tenants' unions. Working within Labour meant navigating the Party's sometimes murky democracy by displaying the weight of support among members (evidenced by the 150-plus local constituency parties who submitted Labour for a Green New Deal's motion to the 2019 Party conference) and persuading the larger general unions (Unite, GMB and UNISON) to join with others, including the CWU (Communication Workers Union) and FBU (Fire Brigades Union), in supporting a programme for climate justice that puts all workers, including energy workers, at its core. This was a moment of historic unity between trade unions and climate activists, with the Labour Party as the vehicle.

In her speech to the Party conference in September 2019, Rebecca Long-Bailey succinctly articulated why many find the Green New Deal so appealing. Building on George Monbiot's argument for 'private sufficiency and public luxury', she told delegates: 'My socialism and your socialism isn't about luck. It's about saving the planet and ushering in a new era of public luxury based on social and climate justice.'

Labour's subsequent election defeat was devastating to all those who had been fighting to prepare the Party to deliver a Green New Deal in government. It demonstrated that there is no easy road to socialism in the UK. Sanders's 2020 campaign remained a source of optimism for a time, until establishment Democrats rallied around Joe Biden's candidacy.

It would be naïve for the left to pin all its hopes for climate justice on the election of democratic socialists in the global North. Had Corbyn become prime minister, those fossil fuel companies whose activities are accelerating the climate crisis would have invested extensively in disrupting rapid decarbonisation. Labour's Green New Deal would have faced resistance from the private interests controlling key infrastructure: transport operators, energy companies, housing developers. National Grid threatened to sue Labour over plans to bring the energy network into democratic ownership.

We must face up to the real possibility not only of further defeat at the ballot box but also of stubborn resistance by capital if and when we do command state power. How then should eco-socialists orient ourselves politically in the 2020s? What is our strategy for winning and exercising power to transform and decarbonise the economy?

Electoralism alone is not sufficient to achieve climate justice, but it remains strategically necessary. In the years leading up to 2019, a convergence of unlikely factors opened up the possibility of socialists winning state power through the Labour Party to deliver a broad suite of social and environmental ambitions. Previously influenced by anarchist ideologies, the climate movement was forced to reconsider the question of state power when it came into contact with Corbynism.

The promise of the Green New Deal is massive state-led investment, regulation and economic transformation, both to decarbonise and simultaneously to guarantee human rights, needs and prosperity. Harnessing state power is the only way to bring about the swift transformations that can halt climate change, and do so justly.

The impacts of climate change are different in character to those of capitalist exploitation and oppression more generally. While capitalism wreaks immeasurable suffering globally, climate breakdown will render our planet irreversibly uninhabitable.

Leading scientists have warned of a 'Hothouse Earth' scenario in which we reach planetary tipping points faster than predicted, as higher temperatures unlock new sources of greenhouse gas emissions through positive feedback loops.* Human efforts to reverse the breakdown would quickly become futile.

The suffering caused by the disruption of our environmental systems will not be evenly felt, but few will be completely immune. Climate justice movements have long made a point of the inequitable global distribution of ecological impacts: while capital in the global North profits, populations in the global South endure flooding, drought and extreme weather events. But recent wildfires in Australia and California, flooding in Yorkshire and South-East England and back-to-back storms across the UK have demonstrated that climate breakdown is an urgent problem for the global North, too.

As liberal governments remain unable to devise or implement proportionate solutions, socialists are increasingly embracing responsibility for putting forward a vision for climate justice. Climate breakdown is now one of the most important factors for those developing socialist strategy to consider.

Interviewed by *Tribune* in the aftermath of the election defeat, Leo Panitch warned that climate breakdown must not be used as a pretext for socialists to shorten their strategic time horizons. He advised activists to 'commit for the long haul' and 'think in terms of ten, fifteen or twenty years'. This is the time-frame required to rebuild working-class organisations, which is a necessary precondition for socialists both to capture and to exercise state power.[†]

---

* Will Steffen, Johan Rockström, Katherine Richardson et al., 'Trajectories of the Earth System in the Anthropocene', *Proceedings of the National Academy of Sciences* 115/33, 14 August 2018.

† Leo Panitch, 'A Decade on the Left', *Tribune*, 7 March 2020.

The tension between the time it takes to build the basis for socialism and the time left to mitigate runaway climate breakdown is excruciating. Socialists cannot neglect the temporality of climate breakdown, but nor can we lapse into frantic, short-sighted strategy. With the Green New Deal we have a plan to mitigate climate breakdown through the same interventions required to build a prosperous socialist society.

Some critics of the Green New Deal have called instead for a politics of 'degrowth', blaming the relentless pursuit of economic growth for the ecological crises we now face. It would be a mistake for socialists to get hung up on reversing 'growth' per se, rather than systematically undoing the dominance of the profit motive throughout the economy by disempowering capital in favour of workers and the public. The COVID-19 pandemic has proved that it is possible to contract the economy quickly, with the effect of dramatically cutting carbon emissions. But as recession follows in its wake, the pandemic also shows that simply shrinking the economy without transforming it is both unjust and insufficient as a strategy for tackling the climate emergency.

In March 2020, the coronavirus crisis swiftly brought the entire aviation industry to the brink of bankruptcy. Virgin Airlines grounded 80 per cent of flights and asked staff to take eight weeks of unpaid leave; Norwegian Air laid off 90 per cent of its employees. Aviation must transition to zero carbon or become almost obsolete, but not like this, with thousands of workers plunged into insecurity.

Carbon emissions have fallen during the pandemic lockdown, but these emissions are the tip of a very large iceberg. Fossil fuels are still the basis of the economy that remains. As capitalism continues to immiserate, it is no coincidence that the crises of climate, inequality and now public health have the same solutions: expanding public ownership right across the economy.

The Green New Deal rejects alienating appeals to climate austerity, which push responsibility for decarbonising onto those least responsible for reproducing fossil capitalism. Moralising won't make individuals change their behaviour within capitalism. A Green New Deal would restructure our economy so that the 'greenest' choice is the cheapest and easiest.

Public luxury means limited private car ownership counterbalanced with free public transport efficiently connecting towns, cities, regions and countries. It means returning land privately enclosed by the rich and powerful to the public, to use for work, recreation and ecological restoration. It means food that is produced, distributed and consumed collectively, rather than for the profits of agribusiness. Such a vision can win majority support for a programme of rapid decarbonisation.

In his viral paper 'Deep Adaptation: A Map for Navigating Climate Tragedy', Jem Bendell argues that we should take a three-pronged approach to the crisis.[*] He emphasises the need for resilience (psychological as well as material), the relinquishment of certain industries and consumption habits (along with other unsustainable elements of civilisation, such as living on coastlines) and the restoration of older ways of life, including rewilding, seasonal diets and non-electronic forms of play.

Bendell has been criticised for overstating the inevitability of social collapse, and his austere, primitivist conception of deep adaptation runs contrary to the mass appeal of a Green New Deal.[†]

---

[*] Jem Bendell, 'Deep Adaptation: A Map for Navigating Climate Tragedy', IFLAS Occasional Paper no. 2, 27 July 2018.

[†] Zing Tsjeng, 'The Climate Change Paper So Depressing It's Sending People to Therapy', *Vice*, 27 February 2019.

But he is right that adaptation has too often been neglected by the climate movement. We should take his intervention as a prompt to develop a socialist politics of adaptation that prioritises justice and is compatible with the optimism of the Green New Deal.

The 2019 report of the Civil Society Equity Review, 'Can Climate Change-Fuelled Loss and Damage Ever Be Fair?', proposed a number of adaptation measures in response to the inevitable impact of climate breakdown. These include: shifting away from intensive agribusiness, renewing mangroves and other forms of natural carbon sequestration, regulating new buildings to withstand future storms, building more flood defences, giving enforceable land rights to indigenous peoples, and tackling underlying social inequalities through technological and financial transfers and capacity building. Such measures could easily be integrated into plans for a Green New Deal.

As environmental impacts become more frequent and severe, measures to ensure equitable adaptation to climate breakdown must become just as central to the demands of climate movements as dismantling the fossil fuel industry and investing in renewable energy technologies. This means establishing that insurance, housing, food, energy, health and social care, education and emergency services are universal basic rights. We should demand the construction or repair of resilient infrastructure, regardless of cost, to protect those rights for anybody at risk. But this adaptation cannot be a new business venture for the same private interests which have profited from taking us this deep into climate crisis. Those at risk of climate impacts should guide the adaptation process through democratic control and public ownership of these services.

Delivering a rights and justice-centred programme of adaptation is obviously not a priority for governments representing the interests of those profiting from climate breakdown. Though we can make demands from opposition, eco-socialists must retain the goal of capturing state power: rather than abandoning conventional politics, we must learn how to buttress our influence by building a more diverse power base from below.

Extinction Rebellion and Youth Strikes have developed innovative models of organising, mobilising hundreds of thousands to push climate up the mainstream agenda. However, neither are organising their respective constituencies around an ideological project – XR is explicitly 'beyond politics'. This is part of what explains their success: a plurality of people can identify with a movement that doesn't contradict any of their core beliefs. Such movements are valuable in asserting the essential truth that the climate crisis is upon us, but they cannot provide alternatives to the current system. For socialists, there exists an opportunity to cohere these existing diverse movements around our own political vision. We should intervene to fill in the political space they create by popularising just climate solutions from our platforms in political parties and trade unions.

Socialists should also use the space created by these grassroots movements to conduct our own community organising. Building power locally will help win material gains and create a sense of possibility around the ambitions of a Green New Deal. For example, the Sheffield branch of ACORN built its base around tenants' rights and is now campaigning to bring local buses into public ownership.

Each of us should take the initiative to identify where social and ecological needs are not being met and work with trusted comrades to fill those gaps. As well as building a diverse ecology of new eco-socialist organisations, it will be essential to restore the power and confidence of the traditional structures of working-class power: trade unions. Our aim should be for unions to treat issues of climate adaptation and just transition as worthy of industrial action.

The FBU is already calling on the government to give fire-fighters a statutory duty to respond to flooding; its general secretary Matt Wrack describes climate change as 'an industrial matter today'. But a renaissance of working-class power through trade unions will only happen if people organise for it. Groups such as Momentum can play a vital role in redirecting the waning energy of Corbynism into the longer-term project of rebuilding trade union power.

This decade will be challenging for socialists, but our movement is the only one with the ideas and organisation to resolve the crises capitalism has birthed. In that, we find hope.

20
Socialist Strategy in the Age of Precarity
Dalia Gebrial

The coronavirus crisis has brought to head a set of contradictions that have been corroding the rights and conditions of the global working class for decades – contradictions to do with work, and related concepts such as worker, workplace and working time. These concepts have been taken for granted by socialists as stable and unifying categories of organisation, but they are being strategically undermined by capital as part of its latest 'fix' for the most recent crisis of accumulation in 2008.

Across the world, we are seeing a dramatic shrinkage in the proportion of people employed in full-time 'standard' work. According to the International Labour Organisation, as of 2019 just 53 per cent of the world's *employed* population are waged, salaried workers – and of this group, 40 per cent rely on informal income streams to compensate for inadequate wages. In turn, more than 470 million people are *underutilised*, meaning they remain precariously tethered to the world of employment: they are not classified as 'unemployed', yet their access to paid work is unpredictable and insufficient to sustain themselves and their families.

Global underutilisation vastly outweighs global unemployment in terms of scale – the former affects twice as many as the latter. Indeed, many countries in the global South have *both* the highest employment-to-population *and* the highest underutilisation ratios in the world – meaning that the global workforce is disproportionately concentrated in the global South, where the quality and stability of work access are worst. So the employment/unemployment dichotomy on which much of our public discourse on 'the economy' relies is no longer the best indicator of whether or not people are able to maintain a materially decent life.

This rise in underutilisation – which is mediated through geographic and sociological divisions of power – comes down to what Gargi Bhattacharyya describes as 'the endless innovation of precarious activities that may or may not constitute "work"'. Capital once promised global integration into the industrial workforce. Instead, it has manoeuvred its way out of the pesky predicament of workforce costs: of providing workers with a reliable salary, sick pay, pensions and the basic means of life. These manoeuvres – which range from legal to cultural to political – combine to undermine and destabilise the figure of the 'worker' as a political subjectivity and an analytical category.

The socio-economic implications of this division between 'the worker' and the 'not quite' or 'sometimes' worker could not have been starker than in Rishi Sunak's coronavirus rescue package. While covering 80 per cent of employees' wages, the initial package did not even make reference to those who work but are not employed. Eventually, following immense pressure from smaller unions, such as the IWGB (Independent Workers' Union of

Great Britain), and then Shadow Chancellor John McDonnell, Sunak finally outlined his plan for those who fall outside the traditional employee model. It was a plan shockingly out of touch with the material realities of these workers' lives. Not only did it leave workers who overwhelmingly live hand to mouth without wages for nearly three months, but it constructed a series of complex bureaucratic hoops through which anxious workers were expected to jump; it also excluded the many workers who build their wages piecemeal from employed and non-employed work. It seems a considerable proportion of Britain's workforce – not, incidentally, comprised predominantly of working-class migrants – simply did not figure in the calculations of policy makers responsible for the economic response to the crisis.

So who are the workers falling through the cracks of employment protections – both during and beyond the crisis? The 'platformisation' of work by the digital gig economy – with its constitutive elements of 'taskification', worker (mis)classification and outsourcing, has been a key mechanism by which capital has accelerated and intensified the underutilisation of swaths of the workforce. These mechanisms are glossed over by the cultural story platforms tell about themselves: they offer 'worker flexibility', and the opportunity to be an 'entrepreneur'. In reality, platform workers are subject to the worst of both worlds: they are not considered employees, and yet are subject to a level of control and discipline by monopoly platform companies that often exceeds that imposed by traditional employers. With no centralised workplace they are dispersed and therefore find it more difficult to connect with one another and conceive of themselves as part of a broader workforce. Indeed, they are encouraged to see themselves not as workers, but as their 'own boss'. The temporal and spatial boundaries between work and non-work are blurred, yet work is broken down into tasks, some of which are compensated and others not.

The composition of the workforces being undermined by platformisation is not incidental. Platform workers are overwhelmingly migrant and/or racially minoritised, and tend to work in key urban and social infrastructural sectors. They are the minicab drivers, couriers, cleaners, carers and sex workers: in other words, the invisibilised backbone of our cities. Excluded from formal workforces, they are pushed into urban centres, where they experience intense forms of structural violence, often racialised and mediated through housing, policing and immigration enforcement.

Racially segmented labour markets have always been critical to Britain's urban development. The most famous example is of course the Windrush generation, where workers from former colonies were recruited into the 'mother country' to rebuild its post-war infrastructure for low wages, and in humiliating working conditions. The displacement of these workers from manufacturing and industrial sectors into unstable, precarious forms of 'self-employment' was exacerbated by the racialised fallout from deindustrialisation in the 1970s. As nations – particularly in the global North – shifted towards a financialised economy, it was black and brown workers who were the first to be shut out from the dwindling landscape of formal full-time work. Today, hostile environment policies manage inclusion and exclusion from the formal labour market by strategically and unevenly distributing precarity through different migrant populations. Once again, race and migration are central to how the state and capital collectively create boundaries not only between the deserving and undeserving poor, but also the deserving and undeserving worker. As has historically been the case, the hierarchical systems that classify human beings into races and workers into strategically defined categories, speak through and alongside one another.

This poses a challenge to socialists, who have often relied on cohesive and clear conceptions of work, worker and workplace in order to organise and mobilise. Big unions are struggling to integrate into their traditional unionising models the growing number of 'not-quite' and 'sometimes' workers, who are transient, politically disenfranchised and spatially dispersed. As the gap increases between the number of available jobs and the number of people needing work, the right is funnelling scarcity anxiety into a culture war between the 'metropolitan elite' and the 'traditional working class', effacing the particular brutality of being working class in urban centres. Following the spectacular failure of mainstream financial and governmental institutions to protect people's livelihoods in the lead-up to the 2008 crisis, the carefully curated image of Silicon Valley capitalists as irreverent and innovative, along with the appeal of 'being your own boss' rather than tied to unreliable institutions, allowed platforms to frame themselves as engines of economic populism. Under what some call the 'entrepreneurial turn' of post-2008 neoliberalism, capital has shifted from trying to break worker power to trying to abolish the formal category of worker altogether.

The future of socialist organising must fully confront the fact that the historical materialist trajectory, in which we all ascend into a unified industrial working class, has not happened and will not happen. Capital is strategically undermining conceptual, spatial and temporal boundaries around worker identity, what is considered 'work' or 'not work' and what the workplace is. How do we conduct workplace organising when there is no clear workplace? How do we defend and build worker power when so many have an erratic and partial relationship to this category? We cannot afford to dismiss these questions as anomalous, when this working model is being rolled out across workforces.

Luckily, we are not starting from scratch. Feminist scholars and activists have engaged with the implications of not having one's work recognised as work – despite its being central to capital accumulation. Campaigns such as Wages for Housework have grappled with the contradictions and difficulties of organising workers who are not considered, and may not even consider themselves, to be workers. Sex worker unions have had to organise in similarly informalised conditions – indeed, some sex workers conceptualise themselves as 'the original gig economy workers'. These campaigns have directly confronted the challenges that come with trying to carve out a cohesive logic of work, worker and workplace, where these categories are not formalised. In turn, there is a long history of 'organising the unorganised/unorganisable' in the global South and among immigrant workers in metropolitan centres for whom precarity and informality have long been the norm. In critical disability studies and disability activism, the profound implications of being constructed as 'unproductive' under capital have been fleshed out and resisted. These models are now central to understanding labour in the twenty-first century, and must be revisited, re-evaluated and reconstructed as part of socialist strategy. Indeed, the imagined norm of the standard, full-time, permanent job was only ever a reality for a tiny portion of the world's workforce – yet it is this assumed model that underpins our conception of 'the working class'.

As twentieth-century concepts of 'work' and 'worker' shift and splinter, the question 'Where next for socialists?' is an open one. Perhaps we attempt to recover and generalise these definitions;

or perhaps we marshal the next crisis of capital into fighting for a post-work future. Most likely, we will have to find some way of reconciling the two. Moreover, as the coronavirus crisis has made clear, the principle of universalism must be revived and centred in everything we do. Capitalism has a funny way of making us feel insurmountably different and distant from one another, while secretly making us more connected and dependent than ever before. Times of crisis reveal the brutal unevenness in how capital is experienced – unevenness that is laid bare in who gets to live and who is left to die. The implications of falling outside the categories that confer safety and dignity, such as 'citizen' or 'employee', and the racialised, gendered and ableist processes that police these categories become stark to those who have taken them for granted.

We must not internalise these processes of differentiation. In the context of climate breakdown, we must make clear that the underlying principle of how society is organised in the next phase of history will be totally oppositional to that which has historically underpinned capitalism: universal access to the means of life. For labour organisers, this does not mean abandoning the category of worker as a revolutionary agent. However, it does mean reconfiguring our relationship to the category of worker, as it becomes more and more inaccessible to the most dispossessed of our world.

21

Against the Austerity State

Siân Errington

The debate about Jeremy Corbyn's legacy as Labour leader, and the future of the left, is taking place in entirely unforeseen circumstances as a public health emergency grips the country and threatens a slide into deep economic recession. The broad realisation that the UK entered the coronavirus crisis with little resilience in the health, social and economic sectors has exposed the impact of a decade of austerity, while the inadequate response of the Johnson government is already prompting reflection upon the role of the British state and for whom it acts.

It is worth recalling just how extreme the UK's austerity programme really was. In *The Shock Doctrine*, Naomi Klein quotes Milton Friedman laying out a core principle of capitalism: that 'only a crisis – actual or perceived – produces real change.' When crisis occurs, those who leap to the foreground with a convincing explanation of the problem and its required solution can transform what previously seemed politically impossible into the only sensible course of action.

Austerity was neoliberalism's response to the 2008 financial crash, with a narrative that turned a real crisis of capitalism (at the time the deepest and sharpest recession the UK had experienced since the Second World War) into a perceived crisis of 'too much public spending' and 'too large' a deficit – a clear and graspable explanation of what had occurred, despite being factually untrue. This sleight of hand successfully laid the blame for a global economic crisis at Labour's door.

Austerity was more than simply 'cuts' to public spending. It used economic language to cloak the political purpose of driving down wages and eroding workers' rights – with well over 3 million now in insecure work – while further skewing the tax system to benefit the very wealthiest even more.* As well as slashing spending on our public services, privatisation was ramped up and extended into areas not previously opened up for profiteering. Social security was restricted and cut to punishing levels, justified through the whipping up of 'scrounger' accusations directed at disabled people. The public investment urgently needed to upgrade our economy, that would have produced a stronger headline economic recovery, was held back.

These measures were accompanied by attacks on civil liberties and the legal rights of campaign groups, charities and trade unions. The tightening of the legal shackles on trade unions through the Trade Union Act 2016 was the most serious attack on the collective rights of trade unions and their members for a generation. This followed attacks on public sector unions over facility time and check-off subscriptions, along with the slicing away of employment rights, for example making it easier to sack

---

* For TUC analysis showing 3.7 million, or one in nine workers, in insecure work, July 2019, see tuc.org.uk.

people.* Many of these and the other attacks came in the form
of a procession of specific, individual assaults against technical
regulations but which taken together exaggerated the exploitative
aspects of our labour market and the growth in insecure work.
As ever, labour market deregulation required increasing restrictions on the collective organisations of working people, the trade
unions. This demonstrates why it is a fallacy to suggest that the
state is ever 'hands off' when it comes to the economy: what
matters is how governments intervene, and on whose behalf.

The cumulative impact of government measures taken under
the banner of austerity meant the deep recession of the financial
crash has been followed by the slowest economic recovery we
have ever experienced. It has meant workers in Britain suffering an unprecedented 'lost decade' of earnings growth. Across
the OECD, only in Greece did wages perform worse in the
aftermath of the financial crisis. TUC analysis found that four
in five jobs created in the first years of the Cameron coalition
were in low-paid industries. Average real wages only returned to
their pre-2008 level on the eve of the pandemic, by which point
8 million people in working households were living in poverty
– having to work more hours (and more jobs), because their
earnings covered less. The impact of years of stagnant wages has
stripped 60 per cent of low to middle-income households of all
savings. Women have borne the brunt of austerity, not just in their
incomes but in their financial autonomy and access to security,
safety and justice. It has also weighed heavily on black, ethnic
minority and migrant communities, who are overrepresented

---

* Changes included extending the eligibility qualification period for unfair
dismissal from one to two years, introducing employment tribunal fees (later overturned) and reducing the statutory period for collective redundancy consultation
from ninety days to forty-five.

in lower-paid roles and targeted by the 'hostile environment' regime, along with the rise in racism.

Overall, the result has been a massive transfer of wealth away from ordinary people and into the bank vaults of the very wealthiest, while at every turn diminishing the power and voice of the majority. The richest 10 per cent hold almost half of Britain's wealth while the poorest half hold just 9 per cent; during an unprecedented lost decade in earnings the gap between the richest and poorest deciles has grown in absolute terms from £1.9 million to £2.5 million.*

While austerity wasn't a new concept for a government using its economic and political power to advance the interests of the few – it did after all build on previous decades of neoliberalism – it was so extreme that it acted as a tipping point enabling 'Corbynism' to break through, with Jeremy Corbyn first becoming Labour leader, then being re-elected and finally achieving an unexpectedly strong result in the 2017 general election. As he told Conference later that year, '2017 may be the year when politics finally caught up with the crash of 2008'.

The optimistic bent of Corbyn's agenda, his authentic record of standing up for peace, social justice and equality, disrupted the neoliberal consensus and set out to change how politics was being done. As part of the ideological dominance of neoliberalism over the last four decades in much of Europe and North America, politics has become increasingly alienating for the public at large, and has instead been practised as an elite sport. Over recent years we have seen the return of mass engagement in British politics; the growth of the Labour Party over this time is to be cherished.

---

* See, for example, *Financial Times*, 5 December 2019.

It has meant more than a Labour Party standing firm against cuts rather than ceding to that framework. It has offered a vision of how a state should intervene into the economy – for the many, not the few, as the slogan went. Under Corbyn, Labour's policy agenda aimed for a decisive shift in the distribution of wealth and power in our society so as to improve the living standards of all, not least in policies such as extending public ownership to embrace the collective, democratic provision of basic human necessities, giving everyone a stake in future infrastructure and widening universal public services. These policies proposed the largest ever extension in individual employment and collective trade union rights. Ideas that had long been popular with the public finally found expression in the upper echelons of British politics.

Since the emotional hammer-blow of the 2019 result, there has been a drive to obscure and distract from the political foundations of Corbynism. But these foundations were well understood by Boris Johnson, who on becoming prime minister cloaked himself in the language of insurgency – the people versus Parliament – to tap into the deep desire for overturning (in any way) the status quo. This was used in the run-up to and during the 2019 general election campaign. The dominance of Brexit as an issue between 2017 and 2019, and the focus on parliamentary manoeuvres, enabled Johnson to paint Labour as part of the establishment. Among wider progressive political layers, the claim that Brexit was the new divide in British politics not only played into this Johnson strategy to a certain extent, but also allowed some elements to re-imagine the Liberal Democrats as part of a 'progressive alliance' despite their direct implementation of austerity measures only a few years before. Meanwhile through 2017 and 2019, as austerity slipped off the headlines, its impact on local communities continued unabated.

As part of this attempt to obscure the political foundations of Corbynism, there have also been efforts to sweep aside discussions about the distribution of power as well as wealth, to present austerity as a matter of cuts, to be solved simply by 'turning the spending taps on'. That is not tenable in the current circumstances: events are putting questions about who benefits from government action, and who carries the consequences of inaction, at the heart of politics. You can see it in the Treasury's response to the coronavirus crisis, in whom the Conservatives intervened to protect first and in who was left hanging. Working from home during the lockdown was mainly a perquisite of the higher paid, while the lowest paid and precariously employed still had to be physically present at work, and face the risks of contagion.

It has become painfully clear that the austerity decade left our public services, communities and households in a fragile state, with little resilience to withstand such a severe social and economic shock.

The coronavirus crisis is likely to be era-defining. It has revealed our mutual dependence and demonstrated the power of the state and the resources that can be mobilised when needed. Corbyn was right to call attention to this in his final appearances as Labour leader.

The combination of the climate crisis, the impact of the austerity decade and coronavirus all make the case – if one was needed – for the profound transformation of our economy through a democratic, transformative socialist agenda. The scars of austerity would – even before coronavirus – have been felt for at least a generation, unless the type of action Corbyn's Labour put forward had been taken. As we undergo a global and national shock much greater than the financial crisis we need to learn the lessons

of the past decade. As a movement we will have to win the argument and prove that our democratic, transformative agenda is
the only one that makes sense. This has to build on the work of
the anti-austerity, left and labour movements in all their guises,
within the Labour Party and outside, rebuilding as a mass movement and becoming part of the social fabric in local communities
and workplaces, as well as gaining ground in Parliament. Over
the last five years, the left has moved beyond campaigning to
prevent things getting worse – rather, we have been developing
concrete proposals and ideas about how to make things better. As
socialists, our resistance to this Conservative government must
continue in the same vein.

22

Where Next for the Transatlantic Left?

Joe Guinan and Sarah McKinley

It was good while it lasted. For a brief shining moment, it seemed as though a new democratic socialist left might be poised simultaneously on the threshold of state power in two of the most important capitalist economies in the advanced industrial world: the United States and the United Kingdom. Writing in the *Nation*, veteran US political commentator Robert Borosage wrote of a new radical progressive politics that is 'on the rise, driven by ideas, grassroots energy, and authenticity', suggesting that between them these forces might 'create a revolution' of potentially global significance.

On several occasions at important historical junctures in the past, parallel political developments in the UK and the US have heralded major political shifts and realignments, setting the stage for enduring new political-economic settlements that subsequently spread internationally. Margaret Thatcher and Ronald Reagan blazed the trail for neoliberalism. Bill Clinton and Tony Blair instituted the Third Way. And so, in the past few years,

socialists faced the tantalising prospect that a new radical transatlantic left might inaugurate another such momentous shift in
global politics.

This new transatlantic left was an odd formation politically.
It emerged from what was, by historical standards, a position of
relative weakness rather than strength. In terms of strategy, it
was the political equivalent of a pole vault attempt, as the movements that coalesced around Jeremy Corbyn and Bernie Sanders
strove for a 'Great Leap over the institutions' (as opposed to a
'Long March through them') in an audacious and opportunistic
grab for the highest levels of state power.* An instinctual rather
than a carefully calibrated move, these efforts always represented
a long shot – a 'Hail Mary pass', in American football parlance –
motivated by desperation at the dire condition of a bloodless
centre-left politics firmly beached by history, on the one hand,
and by the climate clock's unforgiving countdown to ecological
disaster, on the other.

Since Sanders's formal withdrawal from the US presidential
primaries in April 2020, both of these efforts have now fallen
short – although they came far closer to succeeding than even
their most enthusiastic early supporters had any right to expect.
The question now is where this leaves the emergent transatlantic
left – and whether, having run headlong into its first major political defeats, these will prove fatal.

As recently as 2015, the idea that the eyes of the international
left would be turned hopefully on the fortunes of the UK Labour
Party and the US Democratic Party – two of the most deeply
compromised and problematic vehicles for progressive political
change – would have seemed highly implausible, to say the least.

---

*   Edmund Griffiths, 'The Great Leap over the Institutions', 13 December
2019, edmundgriffiths.com.

And yet, this is what has transpired. All around the world, a restless political energy has been searching for an outlet, attempting to find a route to the surface, as evidenced in repeated outbursts, from the Arab Spring and Occupy to the student movement, 15-M and Syriza. The cunning of history is such that it erupted spectacularly in the two advanced industrial economies in which neoliberalism was first unleashed, and where its rot has consequently run the deepest.

In the UK, the beneficiary, against all expectations, was the Labour Party. With the shocks of Jeremy Corbyn's two victorious leadership campaigns, it became evident that a decades-long political ice age was finally coming to an end. The Labour Party's membership tripled, making it the largest left-wing party in Europe. A radical policy programme was rapidly developed and put in place. 'It's been like being in a dark tunnel for a long period of time,' as John McDonnell put it, 'and people are staggering into the light.' When Theresa May called the snap June 2017 general election to annihilate Corbyn, Labour's vote surged, as one shaken right-wing commentator put it, 'in a way we've never seen before', with the Party achieving its greatest increase in vote share since 1945, under Attlee's leadership. Along the way, Corbyn and McDonnell transformed Britain's national conversation, opening up more political space, and in a shorter time, than anyone in living memory.

Meanwhile, across the pond, similarly momentous political developments were afoot. Bernie Sanders's call for a 'political revolution' became an inspiration to a new generation of activists around the country. Following his 2016 presidential bid, the Democratic Socialists of America (DSA) gained 50,000 new members, while Our Revolution – an offshoot of the Sanders campaign – built volunteer chapters across the country in order to drive progressive initiatives, take over state and local Democratic Party structures and elect progressives at all levels. Galvanised by the horror of Donald Trump's election victory over the clapped-out neoliberal centrism of Hillary Clinton, independent groups such as the Justice Democrats have also been helping to organise progressive candidates to challenge conservative Democratic incumbents, while chapters of People's Action – a national network of community organising groups – have been recruiting and running insurgents for state and local offices.

Following the 2018 mid-term elections, in which the Democrats regained control of the House of Representatives, the Congressional Progressive Caucus (CPC) grew to ninety-eight members (about 40 per cent of the Democratic Caucus), and its members chair thirteen major committees, from where they exert important influence and can advance significant reform proposals. Progressive insurgents – most notably Alexandria Ocasio-Cortez and Ayanna Pressley – knocked out longstanding Democratic office holders in the last round of primaries, a warning that other incumbents could not ignore. There is a growing consensus across a broad majority of the country that seeks a bold activist government to address real needs, and the left is on the rise in ways not seen since the civil rights movement of the 1960s.

Corbyn and Sanders have been both central and incidental to the movements that bear their names. Following a long period of technocratic rule by empty suits, it is no accident that radical new political movements in both countries turned to an earlier generation of veteran political warhorses for their standard-bearers. Each in his own way, Corbyn and Sanders are representatives of an awkward squad that was politically isolated by but somehow survived the neoliberal era intact. Their authenticity and moral authority, accumulated over many years, as well as their belief in the power of the collective, allowed them to function as 'servant-leaders' and to embody their movements' demands for economic and political transformation. It remains to be seen whether the movements to which they lent their names will be able to survive their personal political eclipses.

The early promise of the new transatlantic left now appears to have been dissipated in a round of significant political defeats. In the UK, the 2017 general election was a near victory against all odds, but the aftermath was more complicated. On the one hand, the policy agenda and programme for wielding state power accelerated, but its strength also overtook that of the wider social forces necessary to bring it to fruition. On the other hand, the promise of Corbynism as a movement-building strategy following 2017 was not sustained, and the project eventually succumbed to its own weaknesses and contradictions – including getting wrapped around the axle of Brexit by gravitating increasingly towards a second referendum position that cost Labour dearly in its political heartlands.

The devastating scale of the December 2019 general election defeat has dealt the movement a decapitating blow, forcing Corbyn's resignation and severing the vital link between a radical party leadership and the mass membership it had created.

By the same token, the Democratic establishment's unfailing talent for snatching defeat from the jaws of victory should never be underestimated. Hopes that Sanders was in pole position to take the Democratic nomination and carry the fight to Donald Trump in the general election ran aground, the result of an all-out effort by a hidebound and moribund Democratic Party establishment. Democratic elites coalesced around perhaps their least impressive candidate: a barely cogent and visibly impaired Joe Biden, relic of the Obama era with none of Barack Obama's redeeming features.

What transpired in the UK and US amounted to an audacious bid to capture the commanding political heights of two of the most important nation states in the world. If successful, this would have been a heroic shortcut, an opportunistic power grab by the left, bypassing the need for years, if not decades, of hard organising and base-building, to seize the state for the benefit of all.

Where does this leave the transatlantic left? We need to recognise how far we've come and how fast – but also the limitations of our strategies and what must be done to make up for their deficiencies. We are now in a far stronger position than before, however, in two vital regards.

First, we now know our programme. Over the past few years, for the first time in decades, the left began to chart a viable political-economic path forward, through and beyond the multiple crises – economic, political, social and ecological – of our decaying neoliberal order. The new transatlantic left, if it is anything, is a growing coherence around the need for a set of radical structural interventions to change the shape of the economy and the state. Under Corbyn and John McDonnell, Labour developed a necessary and credible programme to undo the damage wrought by four decades of neoliberalism and make the economy work better for most people – for the many, not the few. It drew upon existing democratic economy models as well as a longer-standing left heritage of strategies developed in response to previous crises. Collectively, these strategies formed the mosaic of a new political economy, of which Corbynism became the tip of the spear.

The democratic economy featured heavily in this agenda, with support for insourcing of local public services and further development of the cooperative sector to address local needs that cannot be insourced, as well as a proposal for inclusive ownership funds (IOFs) that would require large companies to transfer 10 per cent of equity to their employees on a collective basis. This tied in with Labour's support for Community Wealth Building strategies, made popular by the success of Preston City Council in developing a new set of institutional relationships – the 'Preston Model' – that keep wealth circulating locally. Labour's economic strategy presented a dramatic shift and rebalancing of power away from corporate finance and the City of London to so-called 'left-behind' regions, communities and ordinary working people.

These ideas were picked up by Sanders and his supporters, who speak freely of public ownership of utilities and propose an even more radical version of the IOFs. Similarly, the Green New Deal (GND) championed by Ocasio-Cortez and others became the basis for Labour's Green Industrial Revolution, which included a proposal for a Green Transformation Fund as the vehicle for a £250 billion spending programme committed to a just transition to an environmentally sustainable economy.

The second way in which we are now in a stronger position pertains to the extraordinary unfolding of recent events. What seemed even a matter of months ago to be definitive setbacks have already been overturned by a world in flux and crisis. The coronavirus pandemic is shaping up to be an even larger economic event than the great financial crisis of 2007–8, with potentially far more significant political and economic ramifications over the long haul.

The economic responses to the coronavirus crisis, quite apart from the true scale of the medical emergency, have torn the veil from the last remaining neoliberal assumptions, radically resetting the contours of politics and of what is economically not merely possible but essential. The state is back, in a kind of reverse *Wizard of Oz* moment. In response to the pandemic, the curtain has been pulled back to reveal, not the shrunken withered state of the neoliberal orthodoxy, but instead the new Leviathan. As we write, our enemies are being forced to consider and even adopt core planks of our programme, not as long-term objectives but as emergency responses.

The new transatlantic left needs to mobilise quickly if we are to continue to shape the direction in which things are moving. We already have many of the policies and strategies this new era requires. Community Wealth Building, the democratic economy, new forms of public-community partnerships and public ownership at all levels, together with a new politics of mutual aid and solidarity – all are critical avenues for action. We must mobilise to demand these policies and show that we can rebuild our broken economies on the basis of a re-localisation and democratisation of economic activity. If we don't, an ugly alternative is on the horizon: a full-on 'shock doctrine' disaster response, combining a new state authoritarianism with ongoing uncontrolled capitalism.

Recent defeats offer us the opportunity to do things properly going forward. Excluded from national-level state power, we are now forced to take the time to do the hard work that was not done in the wake of 2017. We must use the coming years in new ways: for community organising, base and movement building, political education, leadership development and resilience. There is simply no shortcut, no royal road, to the democratic economy. The challenge will be to avoid oscillating wildly, as before, between mutually exclusive poles of electoralism and direct action, but rather to retain the strengths of both and to reach a new, politically effective synthesis.

We must pick ourselves back up and get on with the struggle. We must advance radical self-care and build collective resilience so that we can dig in for the medium term as well as the long haul. Above all, we must practise solidarity in all forms, especially with the most vulnerable, those on the frontlines. In the face of mounting crises, there is an opportunity to grow cooperative networks of mutual care and provision that will strengthen the foundations of the new democratic economy we are already trying to establish. Politics is volatile and history is cunning; the defeats of today may well pave the way for the victories of tomorrow. No matter what, we must be ready to seize the next opportunity to bring about the economic transition that is so urgently required.

23

The Case for Public Ownership

Cat Hobbs

Private companies can do many things well – running public services isn't one of them. Privatisation has failed to tackle the challenges of the twenty-first century: we won't get the decent public transport, green energy, clean rivers, fast broadband coverage or the good hospitals and schools we need without public ownership. And most of the British public know it: public ownership is extremely popular with both Leavers and Remainers, with young and old, across regions, social classes and political divides. Even a majority of Conservative voters want public ownership of rail and water.*

Popular support for public ownership increased substantially during Jeremy Corbyn's time as Labour leader. After forty years of neoliberal consensus, the 2017 Manifesto brought public ownership into the mainstream. By 2019, support for bringing the

---

* David Hall, 'The UK 2019 Election: Defeat for Labour, But Strong Support for Public Ownership', University of Greenwich PSIRU Working Paper, 30 January 2020.

railways and water, Royal Mail and buses into public ownership had increased by 6, 7 and 9 percentage points respectively. This increase in support took place in the context of a constant onslaught from the right-wing media. Every day during the 2019 election, newspapers wrote stories insisting that public ownership would cost too much. That was simply a well-resourced lie. The UK is wasting £13 billion on privatisation every year – money that's going towards shareholder dividends, inefficient fragmentation and the higher cost of borrowing in the private sector.

In the election, we saw what it looks like when a political party challenges vested interests and stands up for working people. The establishment fought back with every means at its disposal to try to stop any redistribution of power – of ownership – to ordinary people. Of course, the day after the election, the share prices of privatised utility companies soared as the threat of a Labour government evaporated. Clearly, we must reform media owner-ship if we're going to get the government and services we need: social media platforms that work for people and democracy, not profit; a properly funded BBC that can be held accountable by its users; and new laws to rein in the right-wing press.

But it is also important to remember how far our campaigning has already shifted the consensus on public ownership. In the 2019 election, while scare stories about Jeremy Corbyn were rife, no one was defending privatisation. Not even the mainstream media could bring itself to defend rip-off rail fares, the pollution of rivers and beaches, the exploitation of care workers, or the corruption of academy headteachers. They weren't defending Richard Branson suing the NHS, excusing the failures of G4S or bemoaning the collapse of Carillion. How could they?

This consensus is clearer than ever within the Labour Party. During the spring 2020 leadership contest, all of the leadership candidates signed up to the We Own It pledge tracker of campaign group We Own It, confirming their commitment to public ownership in ten key sectors: the NHS, schools, water, energy, the railways, buses, the justice system, Royal Mail, council services and broadband. Members and campaigners will, of course, need to hold the new leader Keir Starmer to account for these promises and ensure they are prioritised. But the tone of recent discussion suggests that Labour is finally committed to ending the longstanding con that sees taxpayers' money flow directly into shareholder pockets.

The growing consensus for public ownership has touched Tories too. Northern Rail was the second railway franchise, after East Coast, to be taken into public hands by a Conservative government, even before COVID-19 forced it to implement an emergency rescue package for private rail companies across the country. As *The Times'* deputy business editor Graham Ruddick conceded shortly after the 2019 election, the corporate world has not won the argument on public ownership.

Rail is the classic example of a market failure, but the arguments for bringing rail into public ownership apply to other public services as well. Railways are natural monopolies that deny consumers real choice, and where marketisation therefore fails to drive down prices and drive up service quality; the same argument applies to water and the energy grid. The railway is a network comprising busy central nodes and less busy – but no less essential – radiating spokes, and it therefore makes sense to cross-subsidise investment throughout the network. The same argument applies to buses, Royal Mail and broadband. The ongoing improvement of the railway requires continuous reinvestment as opposed to profit distribution; the same arguments apply to our NHS or to the justice system. Railway operators must be accountable to passengers – just as academy schools or council services must heed parents, teachers and communities.

After the 2019 election, We Own It commissioned new polling to find out why people support public ownership. The two most popular reasons were: people want money to be reinvested in services rather than going to shareholders; and people believe 'privately owned companies prioritise profitable areas over providing a good service to everyone.' Most of us believe that public funding from the taxes that we all pay should go towards improving services. And we understand that private companies running public services have the wrong priorities, cherry picking which services they provide rather than providing a genuinely universal service.

The world changed on election night, as the vision put forward by Corbyn and John McDonnell seemed to evaporate into thin air, much to the delight of the utilities investors. But in the last few months it has changed again. The coronavirus pandemic has shut down normal life and made us feel scared and overwhelmed. Many of us are afraid for our loved ones, many are struggling to get by. The mobilisation of public and private resources undertaken to tackle the coronavirus has been likened to wartime, and while the powering down of the economy is different in crucial ways, the post-pandemic economy, like the post-war economy, will take time to recover and new political space will open up. Once the 'war' is over, the left must create a new narrative from the wreckage, one that does justice to the public sphere.

There are three ways in which COVID-19 creates new conditions for public ownership. First, privatised companies, sometimes entire sectors, are asking for bailouts – we must ensure that conditions are attached, so these bailouts do not serve simply to enrich private shareholders at the expense of people and planet. We should be calling on the government to take over damaging, carbon-intensive sectors such as oil and aviation, with a view to phasing them out over time and replacing them with carbon-neutral alternatives. Instead of giving Branson another bailout, we could offer to make Virgin Airlines a publicly owned company and manage it in a way that helps us meet our climate targets.

As rail franchises come up for renegotiation and renewal, we should push the government to take the operators into public hands. An integrated, efficient railway with reasonable fares and investment in capacity could be a key part of a public transport network that discourages people from using cars and planes. Passengers should have a real say over the long-term vision for our railways, and play a role in holding the public network accountable. Transport Secretary Grant Shapps has indicated that it may become government policy to reduce car use, but this won't happen without planning comprehensive public transport networks. Investment in reducing car use should also be used to create good jobs for the future – more guards to people on journeys, for example, as opposed to unthinking development of driverless cars with individualised pods, which would see society atomised and jobs cut. We have some leverage now over the future of whole sectors of the economy, and we must use it.

Second, UK economic output is forecast to fall by 15 per cent: the entire economy is being reoriented and when the lockdown is over it won't be the same again. In such conditions, people may be more receptive to a positive new vision for our society. The pandemic has forced people to realise that the economy is composed of human beings and that the framework and rules are chosen by us – that we could make different choices. Labour's policy for free, publicly owned broadband, mocked in the aftermath of the election, now looks like common sense as working from home becomes standard. Polling by the *Daily Mail* found

75 per cent of its readers want free broadband during the outbreak. And while Boris Johnson has committed to delivering broadband across the country, the government's own report shows that doing this in the private sector will cost an extra £12 billion. The public sector is clearly best placed to deliver the universal services people need now more than ever.

The left must also ready itself to campaign for a Green New Deal as soon as this crisis is over – because the crisis of the climate emergency is only going to escalate. Green public investment can create hundreds of thousands of jobs in energy generation and in new industry supply chains. Wind and solar power can be delivered almost everywhere in the UK, reversing decades of underinvestment in ex-mining communities decimated by Margaret Thatcher. The art and activism organisation Platform estimates that 40,000 oil workers may lose their jobs by 2030, but that we can create employment for three to four times as many people in clean energy industries. Johnson has committed to quadrupling offshore wind power. He could deliver this by setting up a new publicly owned UK company that creates jobs locally while tackling the climate crisis – instead of leaving publicly owned Danish wind power to lead the way.

Public institutions providing vital services like energy, water and transport, if properly constructed, can help us transition to a Green New Deal and weather the storm of the climate emergency. These organisations should involve citizens, workers and communities in their governance structures, giving everyone a real voice.

Third, the COVID-19 crisis makes it crystal clear – often in heartbreaking ways – that we are all connected. The crisis has created space for a reaffirmation of our collective values – of what's most important to all of us. Protecting human life must

be the priority, as opposed to making a profit. Our NHS wasn't
ready for this pandemic because of years of austerity and privatisation: it was left short of 100,000 staff and 17,000 beds.
Outsourcing cleaning has left hospitals less safe. NHS frontline
staff don't have the protective gear to look after themselves and
their patients, and the government has been scrambling to order
enough ventilators to keep people alive. This was all predictable
but the government decided not to prepare, choosing instead to
continue undermining our NHS.

When the crisis is over, our story must be this: We stepped
up, we volunteered, we helped each other and looked after each
other. We set up mutual aid groups and checked on older people.
Now it's time for the government to do its part. Reinstate our
NHS as a fully public service and fund it properly. We deserve
nothing less.

We must also demand, as Corbyn did, the creation of a new,
public pharmaceutical corporation so we never again find ourselves at the mercy of rapacious drugs companies across the
world when we want to look after our population. And of course
the trade bill and the trade deals that follow it must incorporate
real protection for our NHS and all public services. If the Tories
will not do all this, Labour's biggest achievement when it next
comes to power must be to return the NHS to full public ownership, ending privatisation and outsourcing completely.

Out of the wreckage of COVID-19 we must build a new social
contract that recognises the importance of public services as a
reflection of our collective values – an expression of love, of how
we choose to care for each other as a civilised society. These
services must be properly funded, made to work for people not
profit, and ready to take their place in delivering the Green New
Deal that will be needed before the next crisis hits.

24
Socialism in the Swell of History
Daniel Gerke

Whoever does not feel, in the 2020s, the swirl and swell of history all around has taken self-isolation to an extreme. It is clear that we have entered a new ideological phase of late capitalism, one qualitatively different from what was known variously as postmodernity, the end of history, neoliberalism or the unipolar moment. Few now believe that the normative constructs of that period, from TINA ('There is no alternative') and Third Wayism to Mark Fisher's 'capitalist realism', hold sway as they did before 2008. A sense of contested historicity and futurity has become the cultural dominant, with radical left and right assailing a neoliberal consensus, the material underpinnings of which have been swept aside by successive financial and epidemiological crises.

If there is a single hypothesis which any successful twenty-first-century socialism cannot and should not avoid, it is this: that the age of capitalist realism, during which our collective capacity to imagine non-capitalist realities was blunted by cultural neoliberalism, is over. Now, one could certainly protest that we are still very much inside postmodernity and neoliberalism, and that the 'common sense' of most people still pays generous tribute to capitalist realism. I cannot say with certainty that this is not so, but my contention is that we are in the perfect situation to observe the truth of the Marxist notion that the seeds of any new society are planted in the sod of the old, nourished by its contradictions. Crises multiply and extend as post-capitalist and socialist futures hegemonise the political ambitions of the young.

If capitalist realism is, as it appears to be, being superseded, it remains to discern the elements of lived experience that are making capitalist realism untenable as an attitude consciously or unconsciously adopted by effective majorities of human beings, and making new expectations and assignments of energy not just possible but likely. At this critical moment, socialists must be confident and assertive, oriented towards truth, optimistic about human potential, supportive of human flourishing: they must embody the ethos of a militant, humanist realism.

What should be socialists' red lines going forward into this new contingency? First, we should reject the opposition, borrowed from literary criticism, between realism and modernism; we should be strict philosophical realists while advocating for cultural forms that strike out boldly towards an emergent, speculative future. A reinvigorated sense of historicity and futurity (or 'futurition', as Richard Seymour calls it) must be the imaginative fuel of any modern socialism. We need not rely, in this, upon the cultural modernisms with which we are most familiar: the avant-garde art and literature of the late nineteenth and early twentieth centuries, from the painterly 'isms' to the literary experimentations of James Joyce, Marcel Proust, Virginia Woolf and Franz Kafka. While these forms share with our present cultural dominant the formal character of being responses to overwhelming change, to a clear and present flow of history suffusing artists and their societies, the canon of modernism reflects the experience of a relatively narrow (and well-heeled) group of people within a relatively narrow life-world: the major metropolitan centres of Europe, caught up in the immense industrial, political and sociological ferments of the early twentieth century.

What we must recover and cultivate is what Mark Fisher, in his book *Ghosts of My Life* (2014), mourns as a loss under capitalist realism, namely the social ecology necessary for a vibrant *popular* modernism:

> In popular modernism, the elitist project of modernism was retrospectively vindicated. At the same time, popular culture definitively established that it did not have to be populist. Particular modernist techniques were not only disseminated but collectively reworked and extended, just as the modernist task of producing forms which were adequate to the present moment was taken up and renewed.

Popular modernism, then, was the fusion of formal experimentalism with social critique, made possible by the greatly expanded social accessibility of a 'popular' culture in the post-war world. It opened for working-class people the possibility of expressing futurity, that is, the experience of new and often prefigurative social forms in art and culture. The modernism that I would like modern socialists to champion would comprise: first, the bare political promise of a future, which must nevertheless be fought for tooth and nail; and, second, cultural forms which presage futurity but are neither as broad as current popular culture nor, though they will invariably feel new, as rarefied as the avant-garde.

The next red line for modern socialism should be an ardent humanism. The thesis of the Anthropocene has fully penetrated academia, journalism and the broader cultural discourse around climate change, as well it might. The term is a salient and scientifically justifiable categorisation of our present geo-ecological predicament, but there can also be little doubt that it has contributed to an already pervasive anti-humanism in politics and culture. From pedestrian green cynicism about the human capacity to live in the natural world without destroying it, to worrying signs of an emergent eco-fascism, cultural perspectives on the Anthropocene too often construct *Homo sapiens* and nature as antagonists by default.

Socialists should engage as fully as possible with contemporary writing on the Anthropocene, but from the perspective of a resolute, even a militant humanism. The Marxist theory of history as the development of human social relations (relations of production) in dynamic tension with the development of knowledge and technology (forces of production) is correct in its essentials. This means that history ceases where humanity does. Post-humanism – to be distinguished from a multitude of variably useful reconnections of the human with the non-human, from Donna Haraway's 'making kin' to the provocations of new materialist and realist philosophies – is, quite literally, a historical dead-end. A successful twenty-first-century socialist movement will be a critical friend to projects such as that announced by Paul Mason in *Clear Bright Future* (2019): the 'radical defence of the human being'. We should reject all in-/anti-/non-human futures.

The central claim of all anti-humanisms (where they are not merely condemnations of humanity) is that society, where it is even acknowledged as such, is a machine or system which exceeds and escapes human beings and cannot be said to have its origin in them. This is, of course, a key pillar of neoliberal ideology (deference to the market as a rational substitute for 'society'), now bolstered by the ubiquity of algorithmic systems of control which do indeed appear to 'exceed' human beings. That corporatised algorithms are in fact servants of the ruling class (human beings) and their interests is then a necessary aporia.

Karl Marx's 'commodity fetishism' named just this sense of the social order appearing to exceed human beings, as though 'things' (commodities, including money) were getting on with history without us. In the 1920s, the Hungarian Marxist philosopher Georg Lukács gave philosophical precision to Marx's concept with his analysis of 'reification' – not an ideology, but a psychic effect of the experience of living in capitalist society. Reification prevents human beings from perceiving society as a 'totality' of social relations, from drawing the necessary causal connections between diverse social phenomena and from perceiving the deep motive forces of social change. The most perverse effect is to 'naturalise' society, to make it appear as an externally determined, abstractly objective and thus immovable object, as little interacting with the hopes, dreams and agency of human beings as gravitational waves with the surface of the Earth. As Lukács put it, 'the reified world appears henceforth quite definitively ... as the only possible world, the only conceptually accessible, comprehensible world vouchsafed to us humans'.*

Lukács's theory of reification helps us clarify the relationship between humanism and our cultural sense of historical momentum. Reification is the epistemological effect of a social order which, because it really does dehumanise people (treats them as chattel, extracts their labour, deprives them of autonomy), understands itself to be non-human, to be the product of abstract reason, technology, the market or algorithmic control. The 'end

---

* György Lukács, *History and Class Consciousness: Studies in Marxist Dialectics*, London, 1974, p. 110

of history' marked the high-point of late capitalist modernity's denial of its own humanity, and thus, inevitably, its own historicity. To fight reification, then, is to strive to inject both humanity *and* historicity into the dominant cultural imaginary. This is not merely an intellectual or cognitive endeavour. History is human, but it does not occur inside human minds: it is a real, material undertaking, a clash of forces and powers and a physical mobilisation of interests and demands.

For Lukács, class consciousness is not only awareness of class position ('I am working class', for example) but awareness of: first, how class position is imbricated in a whole human social order (a 'totality'); and second how, precisely because of the structuration of this social order around a class hierarchy, it may be transformed in its essentials only by the power of the working class organised as an advocate for its own interests. By atomising and fragmenting the social order as it appears to consciousness, reification frustrates this awareness.

Working-class people have a good innate sense of class in-itself, their class position, the exploitative basis of the wage contract, the rental contract, the mortgage contract. But the finer details can be explained by Marxists ad infinitum without ever penetrating the armour of reification. After all, what good does it do workers to know they are being exploited if exploitation is simply a natural fact, the price of civilisation, the thing which must be endured 'one day at a time' because 'bills don't pay themselves'? Only praxis, definable for our purposes as activity which punctures the veil of reification, can deliver revolutionary knowledge to working people.

The third red line I have already alluded to: realism. The proliferation over the last several years of innovative work in realist and materialist philosophy – including the speculative realism of Graham Harman, Ray Brassier and others, the 'New Materialisms', and realist and materialist work on the Anthropocene/Capitalocene – has signalled a dramatic weakening of the grip of postmodernist and post-structuralist thought over the academic humanities.

Fundamentally, this is an argument for the reassertion of realist and materialist claims about the existence and nature of objective reality against the pervasive immaterialism of postmodern thought, which has coincided (not by chance) with the period of neoliberalism and capitalist realism. Realism (there is a reality which exists independently of our minds) and materialism (material processes and events have causal priority over ideas) are conceptually inimical to the ideological substrate of postmodern globalised capitalism, and thus also to the specific forms which capitalist realism adopted during the postmodern-neoliberal period. Realism and materialism are symptoms of the end of the end of history; there is nothing antithetical about the real and the modern.

Radical political realism is proving to be a key driver of the recommencement of history. The socialist left, after decades in the wilderness, has re-learned a serious desire to win, and is now planning for victory. Strategy has re-joined ideological debate as a perennial feature of left-wing culture, and with it the rediscovery of socialist theory of a kind which deals directly with power – gaining it, resisting its being taken away, wielding it (a renewed interest in 'state theory' on the Anglophone left is a telling example). The modern left is doing the kind of hard graft which was always necessary, but which, under the great ideological weight of TINA and capitalist realism, seemed futile.

Thus, we have texts such as Mason's *Clear Bright Future*, the 'clear' pointing towards the idea of a transparent road map, drawn out in advance and with care, for future transformations. Rutger Bregman's *Utopia for Realists* (2016) proposes that imagining a better future is quite consistent with common sense and practicality. Radical and programmatic pamphlets have made a comeback, as in Vivek Chibber's *The ABC's of Capitalism* series from *Jacobin* (2018; Chibber also edits a journal with an apt name for my argument: *Catalyst: A Journal of Theory and Strategy*). Meanwhile, thorny questions of socialist construction such as economic planning are once again judged suitable and timely subjects of discussion, as in Aaron Bastani's *Fully Automated Luxury Communism*, Leigh Phillips and Michael Rozworski's *The People's Republic of Walmart* (both 2019) and Sam Gindin's brilliant essay 'Socialism for Realists' (*Catalyst*, 2018). Twenty-first-century socialism, in my view, should be considered a form of the thought and practice of realism at the end of postmodernity.

I hope that the modern socialist movement will *enjoy* exploring the still opaque world beyond postmodernity, beyond the future as 'the same but worse', beyond the dead-end of left melancholia. Ultimately, we will either enjoy excavating the future or we will leave it in the ground. The gambit of modern socialism is that human beings may finally be ready to stop giving up on the history they are unceasingly making.

The successful socialism of the twenty-first century will be ruthlessly and ardently humanist. It will stridently name exploiters and oppressors and proclaim its opposition to a system based on the extraction of life-time from human beings, by human beings. It will engage on the field of political economy with the toolkit of a militant socialism, and on the field of culture with a cultural praxis which reveals the human basis of the social order and the unique power of ordinary people acting together to change it. It will not assume that working people love capitalism, that they've been suckered in, interpellated, conned or made subject; it will instead acknowledge that the prevailing experience of life under capitalism offers no viable or compelling image of rebellion and flourishing. It will then be the task of that twenty-first-century socialism to *produce* that image by facilitating the transformative, self-motivated political actions of working-class people, and in so doing to participate in the human reconstruction of social reality.

25
Culture and Imperialism
Simukai Chigudu

The toppling of Edward Colston's statue certainly made for a dramatic scene. The frantic energy of large crowds cheering while it plunged into the river in Bristol signalled the release of pent-up tension accumulated during a pandemic and widespread anti-racism protests.

Within forty-eight hours, Oxford was seized by the same zeal. More than a thousand people gathered on the city's high street to call for the removal of the statue commemorating the notorious Victorian imperialist Cecil John Rhodes. It was a coordinated, peaceful and impassioned protest about the statue and about structural racism in Britain. When it was my turn to address the crowd, I introduced myself as one of about seven black professors (official statistics are not available) at the University of Oxford, to simultaneous applause and shock. I proceeded to say that I am an angry black man, fully aware of the ugly stereotype that accompanies this image – hot-blooded, impervious to reason and unworthy of serious engagement – particularly when talking about matters of racial injustice.

But how could I not be angry? Like many other black people in the UK and around the world, I witnessed the brutal torture and killing of George Floyd with outrage and revulsion. Outrage and revulsion at the long legacy of structural and institutional racism that has killed, exploited, subjugated and silenced so many black people in the United States, in Britain and in former white-settler colonies.

It is this same outrage at institutional racism that ignited the Rhodes Must Fall (RMF) campaign in South Africa in early 2015. That protest rapidly became transnational, announcing itself in Oxford by asking uncomfortable questions about my university's past. A former imperial training ground, Oxford is strewn with tributes to the great men of the British Empire, who have portraits, busts, engravings, statues and even buildings dedicated to their memory. In contrast, the histories of conquest, famine and dispossession that these men left in their wake are routinely forgotten. RMF drew attention to this iconography as part of a varied agenda that included two additional aims: reforming the Eurocentric curriculums that dominate the university's teaching and addressing the underrepresentation and inadequate welfare provision for black and minority-ethnic staff and students at Oxford. However, it did not take long before all focused on the removal of the Cecil Rhodes statue at Oriel College.

I was a PhD student in Oxford at that time as well as a founding member of our chapter of RMF. As a Zimbabwean, it was difficult for me to view Rhodes simply as a man with views that are odious by contemporary standards, as if it were his words alone and not his actions that were under scrutiny. Rhodes's imperialism gave rise to a pattern of settler colonialism in Southern Africa predicated on racial domination in political, economic and social spheres. In Rhodesia, before independence from colonial rule in 1980, 8 million disenfranchised black people eked out a living at subsistence level or below it, while 250,000 white people, barely 3 per cent of the population, owned more than half of the country's available land, and virtually all of its business and industry. Education, healthcare and housing were all segregated, with white people enjoying standards equivalent to those in Western Europe or the United States.

Rhodes's statue, then, is no mere physical artefact. It is imbued with a noxious history. Its presence at Oriel College reframes Rhodes's conquest as munificence to the university and fails to recognise the exploitation of African labour on which his estate was built. It belongs in a museum, where it can be properly historicised. More importantly, in 2015 and now, the calls for the removal of such statues open up discussions about the dynamics of race and racism, inclusion and exclusion, and being and belonging in Britain.

Initial responses to RMF were hostile, infantilising and casually racist. The Conservative politician and Oriel College alumnus Daniel Hannan disparaged RMF as 'cretinous', dismissed its demands as 'facile' and said that students in the movement were 'too dim' to be at university. Disappointingly, the otherwise astute and justly celebrated Cambridge professor Mary Beard argued that RMF is 'a dangerous attempt to erase the past' and suggested that minority students should be empowered to look at the statue 'with a cheery and self-confident sense of un-batterability'.

Will Hutton, the principal of Hertford College at Oxford, reminded RMF students that were it not for the legacies of the British Empire, South Africa would descend into 'unaccountable despotism' as embodied by then president, Jacob Zuma. Revealingly, apart from a tokenistic nod to Nelson Mandela, Hutton made no acknowledgement of Africans shaping their own political destiny, and seemingly held no conception of Africans as historical agents. As for the upper echelons of Oxford University's leadership, the chancellor Lord Patten conflated RMF with the practice of no-platforming, arguing that students unable to embrace freedom of thought and expression 'should think about being educated elsewhere', even though Patten himself had declined their invitation to debate the issue.

Behind the spectacle of toppling a statue, RMF gained significant traction in the university's student and faculty body, owing to the hard, behind-the-scenes work of a great many student activists. It is a bitter irony then that, for all the exaltation of peaceful protest and deliberative democracy, Oriel College initially refused to remove the statue as it risked losing £100 million in donor gifts from wealthy alumni.

Four years later, we have an opportunity to engage in a more mature and honest conversation about race in Britain. The removal of the Rhodes statue would be a powerful gesture of public accountability and it would allow a good-faith discussion about institutional racism in my university as a small part of much broader demands for racial justice and equality in British society. Numerous writers – the likes of Reni Eddo-Lodge, Afua Hirsch, Akala, Emma Dabiri, David Olusoga and Kehinde Andrews – have already done much hard work in articulating and contextualising the black experience in Britain. Anti-racist activists are channelling years of anger and pain into coordinated protests about Britain's past and present. When the righteous fury and indignation over the present moment begins to simmer down, the messy work of challenging racism in all its structural, institutional and interpersonal guises must continue. But, this time, it will have a greater critical mass.

Postscript

In response to the revival of Rhodes Must Fall and the wider global wave of anti-racism protest, the Governing Body of Oriel College voted on 17 June 2020 to launch an independent commission of inquiry into the key issues surrounding the Rhodes statue. I read the statement with hopeful scepticism. It bore some resemblance to the college's empty pledge to do the same thing back in 2016. However, this time round, the governing body made explicit that its members wished for the statue to be removed. This is a substantial shift in Oriel College's position. At the time of writing, a commission of inquiry has been convened under the leadership of Carole Souter, master of St Cross College, Oxford, and former chief executive of the National Heritage Memorial Fund and Heritage Lottery Fund. While we wait to see the outcome of the commission, the substantive work – that has always been going on in the background – of curriculum reform and improving BAME representation in the student and faculty bodies must continue with even greater momentum.

26
Feminism: What's in a Name?
Amelia Horgan

There are certainties in elections: coaches become battle buses, and journalists who've never been outside London extol the virtues of going to places where people don't know what a macchiato is. But a new certainty has emerged: feminism as a personal brand. A decade ago, centrist politicians agonised over whether to describe themselves as feminists, broadly agreeing to admit they might be feminists but not *that* kind. Now, they are no longer scared of feminism. Rather, centrist politicians are tripping over each other to assert their feminist credentials. Once, feminism meant a commitment to some form of liberatory politics – whether these might have been liberal, radical, socialist or some combination of these. By contrast, Feminism™ is a brand, a public relations operation, a process of personality laundering. It doesn't matter what you've done. You're a woman. And being a woman is good.

Although the leading lights of Feminism™ – Hillary Clinton, Jo Swinson, Jess Phillips – appear decisively beaten, the brand seems unlikely to be forgotten anytime soon. If we believe that a feminism which takes seriously the issues of class, of work, of the relationship between production and reproduction – in short, a socialist feminism – is important, then we ought to consider closely the dynamics of feminism as PR for centrism. The fight for the future of feminism is not one of how to define the term, but for control of a movement on which the hopes and fates of women depend.

Feminism™ shares a great deal with its close relative, corporate-window-dressing feminism. Aside from the crossover in personnel, both share a preoccupation with the ways in which restrictive gender norms prevent women from taking on leading roles in their chosen field, and with the animosity that greets them when they do take on such roles. Feminism™ locates the cause of these problems in stereotyping and inadequate workplace policies for mothers, and finds a solution in networking, supporting more women into senior roles, and creating role models and mentors. As corporate feminist extraordinaire Sheryl Sandberg puts it, 'Conditions for all women will improve when there are more women in leadership roles giving strong and powerful voice to their needs and concerns.' One problem with this account is that it focuses on one group of women – executives and executives-to-be – at the expense of working-class women. While it might be the case that having more women in senior roles reminds the board members that shared parental leave can support women employees, it does very little to help the outsourced cleaner who doesn't even get sick pay. Plus, giving women executives at Big Tech Inc. a better policy on lactation at work will do very little for the women whose children are maimed or killed working in cobalt mines to produce its commodities.

Corporate feminism and Feminism™ share a belief in the foundational goodness of women and the epistemic primacy of experience. Having more women around means better decisions are made for women because women make decisions that are good for women. This might make some sense in the case of the positive benefits for corporate women (although there are also plenty of examples of women kicking away the ladder after them), but when extended to women in general, it collapses. Women in meetings might be able to raise issues that affect women, but women, as of now, have not reached a consensus on what we might do about those issues. How we respond to the problems we face as women, insofar as we can be said to face the same problems, is a question of politics.

Indeed, women often have objectively conflicting material interests. Should we, for example, organise for free, twenty-four-hour nursery care, with decent pay and conditions for nursery workers, or should we offer vouchers to mothers so that they can choose between different nurseries run by academy chains? And can we really claim that the woman running that nursery academy chain and her low-paid migrant employee have the same interests? Women do not have the same experiences, and, perhaps more importantly, they agree neither on the interpretation of those experiences nor on the political questions that emerge from them. Some answers to these political questions are better than others, so what matters is not the mere presence of women, but the presence of a certain kind of politics.

Even though Feminism™ shares with corporate feminism a concern for representation within existing institutions, its adherents are more personally ambitious. Feminism-as-brand isn't about promoting corporate profitability, although it can be profitable: a certain kind of sanitised feminism sells, one that doesn't threaten existing power structures but is instead easily folded into them. Feminism™ is a financial and political grift: a quick route to a book deal, a good way to get on the news. More than this, it allows women in the male-dominated field of politics to position themselves beyond critique. While corporate feminism encourages a narrow kind of feminine business acumen, centrist feminism foregrounds women's vulnerability and fragility even as it stresses their gutsiness. This isn't to say that there aren't gendered, even misogynistic factors at play in the criticism of many centrist women, nor to deny the harassment that they face. Simply being a woman, however, is not an exemption from scrutiny. Nor is it a reason, on its own, for feminist support.

The ambition and grift of personal-brand feminists have often helped other women – for example, through the passing of legislation that has benefited (some) women. But much of their activity also harms women, in two ways. First, the individualism at the heart of Feminism™ pits it against socialism. Of course, the historical relationship between these two movements has not been straightforward, but in the past the battle over their commensurability was at least public and tangible. Personal-brand feminism depoliticises this struggle through its promotion of representation above all else. Second, this new iteration chips away at the theoretical and practical possibilities of feminism. It makes feminism empty, hollow, replacing struggle around the tangible issues of women's lives with the patronising falsehood that having a woman in power always represents progress for womankind. Consider the case of Jo Swinson, who participated in a Tory–Lib Dem government not famed for its support for women, demanding that women be represented in the TV leaders' debates, for women's sake. Or that of New Labour's Yvette Cooper, who described nationalisation as 'switching control of some power stations from a group of white middle aged men in an energy company to a group of white middle aged men in Whitehall.'

Insofar as Feminism™ has any ideological content, its account of power is a liberal and individualistic one. The role of the feminist, its adherents suggest, is to raise her head above the parapet, make people aware of the issues women face and demand reform – though never structural change. In her second book, *Speaking Truth to Power: 7 Ways to Call Time on B.S.*, the recent Labour leadership challenger Jess Phillips writes,

> I would love to advocate overhauling all our slow global systems to make wholesale changes; however, this is an entirely unrealistic [*sic*] and is usually only shouted about by people who do very little to change stuff and just like to whinge.

Instead of wholesale change we should raise our 'authentic voices' and have a savvy social media plan. Although she elsewhere raises the importance of change in the workplace, there is no discussion of trade unions or building the power of organised labour. At times, speaking out becomes all-powerful, the motor of history. At others, Phillips tells us that speaking out 'rarely changes things, but my motivation is always to let others see that it is possible to fight back against bullies'. We don't get a sense of why certain people have power and others don't, nor a sense of how these political inequalities might be challenged.

While the kind of feminism that is discussed in the mainstream press, that is used for centrist feminist personality laundering, and whose slogans are sold in high-street shops, is the heir to corporate feminism insofar as it prioritises individual choices as empowerment, some of its foundational claims have another source: radical feminism. Feminism™ borrows from radical feminism the idea of intrinsically feminine and masculine ways of knowing and being. These ideas are now not uncommon within corporate feminism – particularly in its insipid NGO-development-neocolonial formulations – but they originally emerged from radical feminism. Of course, in their mainstream variant, these ideas lose their bite, specifically their power to re-conceptualise and publicly articulate women's experience of male violence. Take Elizabeth Warren's recent intervention in the Democratic primaries, when she told the Culinary Workers Union that the White House was a 'mess', and that 'when you've got a mess and you really need it cleaned up, you call a woman and get the job done.' Warren was making a joke about gender stereotyping, but beneath the joke is the idea that women are better at just getting things done than men. Femininity is imbued with an almost magical power.

The suggestion that there is a separate feminine culture, a distinct female way of being and unique feminine patterns of engaging with other people and the world, is troubling and ahistorical. It reaches its contemporary liberal zenith in an article by Lauren Duca, the foremost journalist of the anti-Trump #Resistance, in which she argues that the problems of contemporary society are caused by 'toxic masculinity'. She doesn't execute her critique using the radical feminist idea of gender-as-class, in addition to or replacing class as a category rooted in capitalist relations of production, but instead proposes 'toxic masculinity' as an all-powerful force. Her world is organised by feminine (read 'nurturing') and masculine (read 'assertive, pragmatic') energies, with the 'shadow' version of the latter having produced Donald Trump and widespread individualism. Her solution: 'the divine feminine [which] will continue to rise and ultimately defeat the white supremacist patriarchy no matter what'.[*]

Not only does this argument run the risk of essentialism; it fails to pay heed to how gender norms and the institutions

---

[*]   Lauren Duca, 'In Backing Liz Warren and Amy Klobuchar, the *New York Times* Rejected Toxic Masculinity – As We All Should', *Independent*, 21 January 2020.

that inform them change over time. We won't get anywhere by ontologising categories such as femininity and masculinity, painting one as good and the other as bad. We also run the risk of characterising politics as inherently masculine and therefore problematic – in need of *softening*. Jess Phillips, for example, claims that 'to say you are willing to die for your cause is using the masculine language of war'.

A renewed focus on the relations between gender and care has greatly enriched contemporary feminism both theoretically and practically, but the kind of caring feminine divine energy theorised by this brand of feminism is something rather different and much more limiting. As lived and exploited under capitalism, care has a double character: it contains within it the foundation of women's oppression while at the same time opening up new terrains of non-instrumental or even emancipatory ways of living. Appeals to the goodness of the feminine mystify this complex situation and render it one-sided.

Women, their actions and the idea of 'femininity' itself do not exist outside history, politics and power. To secure a better future for women, we need a feminism that can adequately grasp this. We need socialist feminism – that is one that builds sustainable social institutions of women's collective power and of working-class power: a feminism that takes seriously Marx's theoretical contribution, but pushes it to its limits, developing it and creating new analytical categories, rather than treating it with the reverence that a child might do a precious toy. Luckily, socialist feminism – having suffered a double defeat, first to the hegemony of radical feminism in the women's movement and then by the crushing of the organised left by neoliberalism – is finding its feet once again. With the right development of its theoretical and practical energies, it holds the power to change the world.

27

Bridging the Gap:
Corbynism after Corbyn

James Schneider

> *'There is no such thing as Corbynism. There is socialism. There is social justice.'*
>
> Jeremy Corbyn, 13 December 2019

As a distinct body of theory or practice, Corbynism may not exist. Neither reading groups nor revolutionary parties will bear that name. But what was this distinct and vertiginous period of socialist advance and eventual electoral defeat? And more importantly, what now for the half-orphaned movement that rode a great, exhilarating wave of possibility?

All the participants in Jeremy Corbyn's 2015 leadership campaign will admit that the surge in support took them by surprise. In May 2015, the leader of the Labour left and later Corbyn's campaign chair, John McDonnell, proclaimed that moment 'the darkest hour that socialists in Britain had faced since the Attlee government fell in 1951'. Three weeks later, Jeremy Corbyn was on stage with the three New Labour continuity candidates at Newsnight's televised hustings, visibly winning over an audience of former Labour voters in Tory-held Nuneaton with his unpolished message of peace, public ownership and democracy.

The mechanics of how Corbyn catapulted from 200–1 outsider to leader of a semi-hollowed-out party have been well covered, most notably by Alex Nunns in his excellent book *The Candidate* (2016). Suffice to say the campaign wasn't won because the Labour left was well organised and prepared for success. Rather, a wave from below powered the campaign, and Corbyn rode it to the finish line. Crucially, that wave wasn't an expression of the power of the UK's organised progressive forces – the labour, peace, anti-racist, feminist, anti-austerity, ecological and tenants' movements, along with critical culture, media, class consciousness and social solidarity – although Corbyn's campaign was an expression of their interests, talents and energy. It instead demonstrated the fragility of their opponents: the ruling class and its witting and unwitting agents of control.

While the basic coordinates of the economic and political system were unchanged following the 2008 financial crisis, the status quo was at its most open to challenge in a generation. The 2015 British Social Attitudes survey found that over half of the British public thought the government does not much care what 'people like me think'. The 2016 survey showed close to half the population supported higher levels of spending on health, education and social security. Dissatisfaction with the status quo, though inchoate, was all around.

But the political-media class looked at the majority won by David Cameron's Conservatives in the 2015 general election – 11.3 million votes, 37 per cent of the total – and saw an endorsement of the status quo. The columnists and focus group pedlars weren't looking at what was hiding in plain sight. UKIP's 4 million votes, the SNP's near clean sweep in Scotland, support for Scottish independence, the Green Party's rapid pre-election membership growth and the expansion and vitality of the anti-austerity and student movements all showed there was energy for change, bouncing off in many directions. It awaited an effective vehicle to cohere and unlock it.

'We don't have to be unequal. It doesn't have to be unfair,' Corbyn proclaimed in his acceptance speech following the 2015 Labour leadership election. 'Things can, and they will, change.' This powerful statement of possibility filled the lungs of socialists and progressives across the country. It also revealed a weakness: who would do the changing? The expression typified the central challenge for the Corbyn project. Yes, the system was struggling to reproduce itself, but no, we were not the cause. Between the circumstances of systemic fragility and the relative weakness of progressive social forces opened a gap – which Corbynism occupied.

The Corbyn project's task was to occupy that gap for as long as possible while closing it by building up progressive social forces. This task was enormous: forty years of defeat for the left had fundamentally reshaped society. The Labour Party was cartelised, local government hollowed out and Westminster insulated from pressure from below. Tenants were stripped of protections and a voice. The peace, anti-racist, feminist and ecological movements advanced, but struggled to join forces. And the once-powerful organised working class was reduced to a residue, as the wage share of national income fell from almost two-thirds to just over half. The balance of forces was decidedly unfavourable.

Corbyn's leadership offered an opportunity to arrest this historic decline and lead a new advance. But to spur on a movement while desperately hanging on to office was a colossal task. Corbyn's allies were few: three fellow members of the shadow cabinet; less than a tenth of Labour MPs; an understaffed office; a new organisation, Momentum, which had no money, governance structures or agreed strategy; and a relatively weak organised trade union and social-movement left. The mass of the membership and the weight of Unite, at least, were on his side. The scale of hostility he faced from the media and Labour's anti-socialists, on the other hand, was extreme and unprecedented. John McDonnell liked to reference the Gramscian concept of struggle 'in and against the state'. Before Corbyn got close to Downing Street, he would have to struggle 'in and against the Party'.

In the summer of 2016, the anti-socialists committed a great mistake: by orchestrating an attempted coup, they allowed the unorganised forces supporting Corbyn to join forces with Unite and Momentum. The 2016 leadership campaign didn't just increase Corbyn's mandate, securing the project's continued occupation of the gap; it also reduced the gap by further strengthening, educating and organising progressive forces around a common project for power.

A similar pattern repeated itself in the following year's general election. Corbyn's campaigning skill, the Party's popular policies and the quirks of British electoral broadcasting rules, which focus attention on parties' top leaderships, drew a new, defining antagonism: Corbyn's Labour against austerity Conservatives. That allowed Corbyn to be heard on issue after issue advocating popular social-democratic policies. Just two years before, such strategies – scrapping tuition fees, ending austerity, taking utilities into public ownership, increasing taxes on the rich – had been politically marginal. In 2017 they re-entered the mainstream.

Labour's 13 million votes didn't secure victory, but the largest vote share increase since 1945 kept Corbyn in office and dramatically shifted political discourse. The campaign organised, educated and empowered the movement, which began properly to contemplate government for the first time. The gap between possibility and power closed substantially.

At Labour's September 2019 conference, the membership moved to the left of the leadership, pressuring progressive policy change from below. But such grassroots power was felt unevenly across the Party. MPs remained hostile, but a socialist majority had taken the National Executive Committee and appointed a socialist, Jennie Formby, to head up the Party bureaucracy. Several socialist cadres were hired and Momentum's staffing numbers grew on the back of its 40,000-strong membership, swelling experience and capacity on the left.

Change came slowly in most regional offices and in the Party's elections department, which fiercely resisted the formation of a new Community Organising Unit that was central to a long-term socialist strategy. More Labour councils were trying to deliver municipal social democracy by 2019 but local government was still far from a site of socialist hope and resistance.

Reforms to how MPs are selected by local parties were a flop, and the Party's Democracy Review democratised little. But Momentum, Unite and the CWU (Communication Workers Union) successfully won the selection of left candidates in about half of Labour's target seats. However, the 'preparing for government' exercise was, while detailed, fatally flawed. It tended to treat Corbyn's programme as something that could be implemented by existing state machinery, without mass mobilisations, and that would face little establishment backlash.

If party reform tended to be top-down, political education would have to come from below: neither the Party nor

Momentum nor Unite put together a substantial programme. Proposals for turning Young Labour into a 'university of the working class' never got off the ground. But The World Transformed had become the most vibrant part of the conference each year and spawned a number of local festivals across the country. The horizon of state power turbocharged the Corbynite intellectual space: several important books were published in 2018 and 2019; *Tribune* and Novara expanded their output; and a boom in left-friendly think tanks developed.

In the economic realm, the Corbyn period saw a limited advance for progressive forces. After decades of decline, trade union membership stopped falling and then began to rise – although overall membership still skews towards public sector, better-paid and older workers – and trade unions have been substantially relegitimised in public discourse. Although organisations such as ACORN, Generation Rent and the London Renters Union have made progress, we are still a long way off a national tenants' movement.

No new working-class social institutions have replaced the past's dense lattice of everyday solidarity. But while media hostility remained intense, often to the point of absurdity, more socialist voices and perspectives were included in current affairs programming. Public discourse and political common sense as a whole shifted, though critical mass culture on television and radio is much rarer than it was in the 1970s. Grime, a genre whose artists and fans broadly backed the change that Corbyn offered, was one bright spot, providing anti-establishment messages – 'Fuck the government and fuck Boris,' as Stormzy raps in chart-topping 'Vossi Bop' – for mass audiences.

The peace, anti-racist and feminist movements all remained energetic, even as a number of their activists were drawn into

Labour-focused work. The ecological movement advanced dramatically during Corbyn's tenure, but (notwithstanding his sincere and longstanding personal commitment to environmentalism) not because of it. Indeed, Labour was quiet on environmental issues until 2019, when – under tremendous pressure from below, from youth climate strikers, Extinction Rebellion and Labour for a Green New Deal – it took an impressive leadership role, developing and championing ambitious policies. This striking shift in direction and tempo revealed the possibilities for a party porous to movement demands.

All considered, the progressive movement inside and outside the Party was substantially more developed on the eve of the 2019 general election than it had been in 2017 or 2015. This capacity was evident in the campaign, where the elements of the party machine that weren't hostile to the members and Momentum organised an impressive number of campaigners. At the moment of electoral mobilisation, the movement was strong, but the leadership had run out of steam, worn down and fractured by Brexit.

In two and a half years of battles on the issue, Corbyn never found ground he could hold. Usually on the retreat, he was left arguing for compromise for its own sake, with the Brexit policy defined by neither socialist principle nor strategic electoral viability. Brexit gave the establishment a wedge to drive into the heart of the Corbyn project – and it did so with glee. Its repertoire – round-the-clock attacks, accusations of idiocy, performative confusion – need not be rehearsed. Within the Party, those who both supported Corbyn and wished to overturn the referendum result acted in large part as the establishment's unwilling dupes. They wanted Corbyn to make the anti-democratic, Europhile argument that he never convincingly could. By the 2019 general election, Corbyn had lost his room for manoeuvre and his team was fundamentally divided on how to play an extremely challenging hand. The burnish of 2017, when Corbyn had appeared a politician apart, authentically himself, had been painfully wiped off.

In 2017, by focusing on a class antagonism and offering a set of popular policies, Corbyn's Labour controlled the left, sweeping aside the social reformers and liberals. In 2019, Labour won 10.3 million votes, more than in five of the last ten general elections, but fewer seats than in any since 1935. The discrepancy can be explained primarily by the semi-floating signifier of Brexit. Boris Johnson's Conservatives brutally and effectively dominated the right by purging and otherwise sidelining Conservatives squeamish about the government's Brexit strategy and cajoling the Brexit Party to stand down in every Tory-held seat. Europe was the defining issue, and the Conservatives' 'Get Brexit Done' slogan brought together diverse voter groups – pro-Leave, anti-politics and those weary of the Brexit debate. Labour was left promising that substantial change could come through the ballot box, just not the substantial change a majority voted for in 2016.

With Corbyn's tenure over, Labour will not immediately return to offering tepid social reform, but nor will its leadership fight for socialism. Keir Starmer is neither a ghoulish neoliberal, nor a reactionary authoritarian, nor a lover of war, but he isn't a socialist. Hard to place, he appears to be on the progressive end of social reformism, the nicest possible part of the establishment. He has no strong allergy to being near socialist ideas, but they aren't to his taste or style.

The situation should not cause socialists to despair. Labour is not and never has been a socialist party. But over the last four and a half years, socialist leadership has provided a project for power for progressive forces to work towards. The challenge for these forces is to keep growing – and all pull in roughly the same direction – now that there is little leadership and no single strategic horizon.

After the compressed focus of the Corbyn era, a great variety of strategies will re-emerge. The process could and likely will prove messy. Sectarianism, particularism and cultural differences will reassert themselves. But a multiplicity of strategies need not be disastrously divisive; in fact, it's necessary. No one has a monopoly on wisdom – and a fog covers the path to sustainable socialist advance.

Some will focus on greenfield industrial organising, democratising trade unions, defending the socialist position in the Labour Party or direct action. Others will concentrate on feminist activism, community organising, anti-racist work, the climate emergency, the cultural terrain, challenging imperialism, cooperation between anti-Conservative parties or organising tenants. If these different strands butt against each other and fracture the movement, then the gap between the relative strength of progressive forces and the ruling class is likely to widen. But if they broadly run in the same direction and there is a degree of coordination between them, such progressive forces could be strengthened, preparing the ground for the next major opportunity for advance.

Here, Momentum could play a vital role if it commits to change and evolves. After a necessary process of renewal and re-democratisation, the organisation could articulate a socialist strategy in the Party and in society connecting with all of the efforts above. With no party leadership to defend, Momentum could focus on bridging the gap between the moment's possibility and the movement's weakness. It could help build socialist capacities across the movement as a whole and offer coordination on every terrain of social struggle.

The Corbyn movement may be half-orphaned but it is no infant. It can succeed if it proves its maturity through tolerance for diversity, internal generosity and commitment to the long haul. Corbyn's leadership was never going to bring socialism, even if elected with a majority government. It was a spark, an organiser and a staging post. It is up to the movement to take the cause further and win advances, for the many, not the few.

The movement can prove Jeremy Corbyn right: there is no such thing as Corbynism. There is socialism. And things can, and they will, change.

Contributors

Sita Balani is lecturer in contemporary literature and culture at King's College London. She is co-author of *Empire's Endgame: Racism and the British State* (Pluto Press, 2021) and author of *Deadly and Slick* (Verso, forthcoming).

Gargi Bhattacharyya is author of *Rethinking Racial Capitalism* (Rowman & Littlefield, 2018) and *Crisis, Austerity and Everyday Life* (Palgrave, 2015) and is co-author of *Empire's Endgame* (Pluto, forthcoming 2021).

Grace Blakeley is a staff writer at *Tribune* and author of *Stolen: How to Save the World from Financialisation* (Repeater Books, 2019).

Simukai Chigudu is associate professor of African politics at the University of Oxford and author of *The Political Life of an Epidemic: Cholera, Crisis and Citizenship in Zimbabwe* (Cambridge University Press, 2020).

Siân Errington is a political officer at the Unite trade union. She advised on policy for Jeremy Corbyn's 2016 leadership campaign.

Cristina Flesher Fominaya's latest book is *Democracy Reloaded: Inside Spain's Political Laboratory from 15-M to Podemos* (Oxford University Press, 2020).

Dalia Gebrial is a PhD candidate at the London School of Economics and on the board of the journal *Historical Materialism*.

Daniel Gerke is a researcher at Swansea University and blogs at anthromodernism.wordpress.com. He is writing a book about Raymond Williams for University of Wales Press.

Jeremy Gilbert is professor of cultural and political theory at the University of East London. His books include *Twenty-First Century Socialism* (Polity, 2019) and *Hegemony Now: Power in the Twenty-First Century*, with Alex Williams (Verso, forthcoming).

Sam Gindin is the co-author, with Leo Panitch, of *The Making of Global Capitalism: The Political Economy of Empire* (W.W. Norton, 2020) and co-author, with Leo Panitch and Steve Maher, of *The Socialist Challenge Today* (Merton Press, 2019).

Joe Guinan is a senior fellow at the Democracy Collaborative in Washington, DC, and co-wrote *The Case for Community Wealth Building* (Polity, 2020).

Owen Hatherley is the author of several books, including *Landscapes of Communism* (Allen Lane, 2015), and is the culture editor of *Tribune*.

Tom Hazeldine's *The Northern Question: A History of a Divided Country* is published by Verso (2020).

Cat Hobbs is the founder and director of We Own It, an organisation that campaigns against privatisation and for public ownership.

Amelia Horgan is writing a PhD thesis on the philosophy of work. Her first book, *Lost in Work: Escaping Capitalism*, will be published by Pluto Press in spring 2021.

Ashok Kumar is lecturer in international political economy at Birkbeck, University of London, and author of *Monopsony Capitalism: Power and Production in the Twilight of the Sweatshop Age* (Cambridge University Press, 2020).

Rory MacQueen was chief economic advisor to Shadow Chancellor John McDonnell.

Sarah McKinley is director of European Programmes at the Democracy Collaborative, based in Brussels.

James Meadway is a former chief economist at the New Economics Foundation and was an advisor to Shadow Chancellor John McDonnell.

Keir Milburn lectures in political economy and organisation at the University of Leicester and is the author of *Generation Left* (Polity, 2019).

Tom Mills is a sociologist at Aston University. His book *The BBC: Myth of a Public Service* appeared in 2016 (Verso).

Andrew Murray is chief of staff at the Unite trade union, and author of *The Fall and Rise of the British Left* (Verso, 2019).

Leo Panitch is professor emeritus at York University, Canada, and co-editor of *Socialist Register*. His most recent book is *Searching for Socialism* (Verso, 2020), with Colin Leys.

Richard Pithouse is editor-in-chief of *New Frame*, South Africa coordinator for Tricontinental: Institute for Social Research and Associate Professor at the WiSER, University of the Witwatersrand.

Vijay Prashad is executive director of Tricontinental: Institute for Social Research and author of, among other things, *Red Star over the Third World* (Pluto, 2019).

Palagummi Sainath is the founder of the People's Archive of Rural India and author of *Everybody Loves a Good Drought* (Penguin, 1996).

Chris Saltmarsh co-founded Labour for a Green New Deal. He is writing a book about climate justice for Pluto Press (2021).

James Schneider volunteered on Jeremy Corbyn's 2015 leadership campaign, co-founded Momentum and served as Labour's head of strategic communications.

Rory Scothorne is a doctoral student at the University of Edinburgh and a co-author of *Roch Winds: A Treacherous Guide to the State of Scotland* (Luath, 2016).

Lola Seaton is an assistant editor at the *New Statesman*.

Joshua Virasami is an organiser and artist whose book *How To Change It* is published by #Merky Books (2020).